THE BATTLE OF BRITAIN

by IRA PECK

SBS SCHOLASTIC BOOK SERVICES
New York Toronto London Auckland Sydney

Photo Credits

United Press International: Pages 6, 9, 10, 14, 24, 26, 27, 32, 37, 38, 40, 42, 46, 51, 52, 57, 78, 82, 86, 101, 106, 108, 112, 118. Wide World: Pages 7, 12, 21, 28, 32, 43, 52, 66, 119, 120. Brown Brothers: Page 15. Imperial War Museum: Pages 18, 19, 23, 52, 55, 72, 77, 80, 87, 92. Gilloon: Pages 97, 114-115, 122.

Passages quoted on pages 76-79 and 89-91 are from *Icare* magazine. Used by permission.

Passages quoted on pages 98-102 and 115-117 are from *The Winter of the Bombs* by Constantine Fitz Gibbon. Reprinted by permission of Harold Ober Associates Incorporated. Copyright © 1957 by Constantine Fitz Gibbon.

3rd printing . . . . July 1970

Printed in the U. S. A.

CONTENTS

I. "THEIR FINEST HOUR" 5

II. BOTH SIDES PREPARE 11

III. BRITAIN STANDS ALONE 25

IV. HITLER HESITATES 39

V. THE AIR BATTLE BEGINS 47

VI. THE ATTACK OF THE EAGLES 67

VII. THE LUFTWAFFE ALMOST WINS 81

VIII. THE BATTLE REACHES A CLIMAX 93

IX. LONDON'S ORDEAL—"THE BLITZ" 113

X. WHY BRITAIN WON 125

CHAPTER I
"THEIR FINEST HOUR"

We call it now, almost 30 years later, the Battle of Britain, and we know it was a famous victory. Perhaps we can even quote some of Winston Churchill's words about it or, at least, try to. But for many who lived at the time, memories are short, and those who were born afterward can hardly be blamed for not knowing much about it at all.

Oddly enough, at the time of this epic World War II battle, the men who fought it had little idea of its importance. It is very unlikely that any Royal Air Force fighter pilot ever said, or even thought, "I am fighting the Battle of Britain and on its outcome depends the fate of the world." If he *had* said it, he would have been booted in the pants and become the laughing stock of the R.A.F. The fact is, the average fighter pilot at the time just thought he was doing his everyday job. It was not because of a false sense of modesty. He simply could not know then the historic nature of the struggle. Winston Churchill, the British Prime Minister, knew it. His Cabinet knew it. So, too, did his top military commanders. But the men who fought it, no.

This is what Squadron Leader James H. "Ginger" Lacey said about it recently:

"At the time, we didn't know that it was a vital battle. We thought that that was the way a war was fought. You know — it was fighting every day and you just carried on. We didn't know we were quite so close to defeat, either.

Left, top: "Ginger" Lacey in 1940. **Below:** Lacey and Peter Townsend, another Battle of Britain ace, in 1969.

British Spitfires patrol the sky early in World War II.

Because down at squadron level, pilot level, we didn't know how short we were of aircraft and of pilot replacements.

"We didn't have the overall picture. Churchill had the overall picture and *he* knew at the time that it was going to be the crucial battle of the war as far as Britain was concerned. If we'd gotten down to it and thought about it, it would have been apparent to us, too, but we were just young boys. I was 23, and I was one of the experienced ones. Most of the pilots were even younger."

What then was the Battle of Britain, and why was it so crucial? As a battle, it was a decisive but fleeting moment in history, one that will never be repeated. It was a time of great air battles fought by manned aircraft. In a way, these

German troops disarm Polish prisoners of war in Warsaw.

air battles were not unlike the aerial "dog fights" of World War I, but on a much larger scale and using much more advanced weapons. The days of such air battles were numbered from the time in 1944 when the Germans began hitting London with supersonic missiles. If there is another great war, intercontinental missiles with nuclear warheads will probably be the ultimate weapon, and the manned fighter and bomber, the main participants in the Battle of Britain, will be as obsolete as the horse-drawn trolley car.

The question of *why* the Battle of Britain was so crucial was answered for all mankind by Winston Churchill on June 18, 1940. On that grim day, Britain, its army practically bare of the heavy weapons of war, stood virtually alone

7

against the overwhelming might of Nazi Germany. The armies of Adolf Hitler, the ruthless German dictator, had smashed through Holland, Belgium, and France, and were now the prison-keepers of Europe. The British army had been driven off the continent, though most of it had survived to fight another day. Winston Churchill rose in Parliament that day, June 18, to rally his countrymen against the so far invincible enemy. These were the last sentences of his address.

"The Battle of France is over. I expect that the Battle of Britain is about to begin. Upon this battle depends the survival of Christian civilization. Upon it depends our own British life, and the long continuity of our institutions and our Empire. The whole fury and might of the enemy must very soon be turned against us. Hitler knows that he will have to break us in this island or lose the war.

"If we can stand up to him, all Europe may be free and the life of the world may move into broad, sunlit uplands. But if we fail, then the whole world, including the United States, will sink into the abyss of a new Dark Age made more sinister . . . by the lights of perverted science. Let us therefore brace ourselves to our duties, and so bear ourselves that, if the British Empire and its Commonwealth last for a thousand years, men will say, 'This was their finest hour.' "

Churchill at that moment was looking into the future. We, nearly 30 years later, can look back and see that he was right about almost everything. The Battle of Britain was indeed about to begin. It *would* be Britain's "finest hour." And eventually it *would* cost Hitler the war.

Winston Churchill gives his famous V-for-victory sign.

CHAPTER II
BOTH SIDES
PREPARE

Historians and writers seldom agree about the details of any battle, and the Battle of Britain is no exception. When, for example, did it begin? The Germans usually say it began on August 13, 1940. This day, which they called *Adler Tag* (Eagle Day), marked the beginning of a great air offensive designed to destroy the R.A.F.'s fighter force. The British usually say that the Battle of Britain began on July 10, when German aircraft began pounding ship convoys in the English Channel. The British date is actually much closer to the mark. Yet one could just as easily say that it began a few days sooner, or later, and not be wrong.

One could also say that the Battle of Britain began many years before and not be wrong, either. Germany began a huge buildup of its Air Force — secretly, at first — immediately after Hitler took power in January, 1933. Britain began to meet the threat in July, 1934, when it became aware, from intelligence reports, of the German buildup.

Yet the Germans had not been idle even in the years before Hitler. The Treaty of Versailles, which officially ended World War I, forbade Germany to have an Air Force. The German High Command, however, was fairly ingenious at getting around this. As early as 1921, it began forming the nucleus of the future *Luftwaffe* (Air Force). It managed to train future military pilots secretly in civil aviation schools. Other military pilots were trained in a secret school set up in Lipezk, Russia, from 1928-1931, with the

Adolf Hitler struck this Napoleonic pose around 1933.

Gliders helped train future Luftwaffe pilots in 1920's.

approval of the Soviet government. In 1926, a commercial airline, *Lufthansa*, began operating in Germany. Its schools and pilots also lent themselves to secret military training, while its airfields and other facilities were quite capable of a double use. It was hardly a coincidence when the first chairman of *Lufthansa*, Erhard Milch, later became the No. 2 commander of the German Air Force.

German aircraft manufacturers were limited to producing commercial planes, but some of these could easily be converted into bombers, and some actually were later on. Denis Richards, author of *Royal Air Force 1939-1945*, tells the story of a German worker who stole, piece by piece, all the parts of a baby carriage from the factory in which he worked. When he put them together at home, they came out a machine gun. Similarly, Richards says, German civil airliners kept coming off the production lines as potential bombers.

There was also another way that Germany could — and did — train future military pilots. One of the most popular "sports" in Germany after World War I was gliding. By 1929, there were thousands of well-organized glider pilots in Germany, many of whom easily made the step to secret military training.

When Hitler took power in January, 1933, Germany already had an experienced, though secret, Air Force of some 20,000 men. Germany had, however, no purely military planes. Hitler swiftly changed all that. In violation of the Versailles Treaty, he spurred the German aircraft industry to a vast expansion program. By 1934, military planes were coming off the production lines at the rate of 160 a month. Early in 1935, Hitler felt secure enough to lift the veil of secrecy from his Air Force, naming Hermann Goering, the No. 2 Nazi leader, its commander-in-chief. Goering's qualifications for the job were that he had been a World War I fighter pilot and was an old political crony of Hitler's. Though Goering had no real qualifications for the job of commanding the Luftwaffe, the thought apparently never entered Hitler's mind. But then it never occurred to Hitler that he, a former World War I corporal, had no qualifications to be the Supreme Commander of Germany's armed forces, either.

What was Britain doing all this time? After World War I, there was a natural tendency toward disarmament and economy in that country. In 1934, when German aircraft production was beginning to zoom upward, the R.A.F. was little more than a skeleton force. At that time, it had about 488 planes for the defense of Britain, and most of them were bombers. They were practically all wood and canvas biplanes, similar to those used in World War I, and were already obsolete. Britain's best fighter was the Fury II, a bi-

Luftwaffe chief Hermann Goering liked ornate uniforms.

plane armed with two machine guns and capable of about 223 miles an hour.

In July, 1934, a motion was introduced in Parliament to increase the size of the Royal Air Force by 41 squadrons. (The average squadron had about 16 planes, of which 12 were usually serviceable, the rest being grounded for inspection and repair.) By this time, the British government was well aware of the rapid expansion of Germany's Air Force, and this was its answer. There was some opposition in Parliament to the proposed increase. Was it really necessary? What was the danger that required it?

At that point, the Member for Epping, Winston Churchill, rose to answer the opposition. Churchill began by pointing out just how vulnerable England was to air attack. He called London "the greatest target in the world, a kind of tremendous fat cow tied up to attract the beasts of prey." The danger to Britain, he said bluntly, came from Ger-

Goering inspects a Luftwaffe honor guard in Berlin.

many. Then he began to give "some broad facts" which he challenged anyone to contradict. Churchill's "facts" were drawn from his own private intelligence sources, and while not 100% accurate, were close to being so. Churchill said that the German Air Force, built in violation of the Treaty of Versailles, was already nearly two thirds as strong as Britain's home defense force. In this, Churchill erred somewhat. *Numerically* the Luftwaffe was about two thirds as strong, but organizationally it was not. Churchill's other information proved to be remarkably sound. He predicted that by 1935 the German Air Force would nearly equal Britain's home defense force and by 1936 would be much stronger. Finally, he said, once Germany had taken the lead, it might never be overtaken. All of these predictions came true.

Parliament voted to expand the Royal Air Force, and from that point until the outbreak of war on September 1,

1939, the race for air supremacy was on. In numbers, the Germans far outstripped the British. The reason was simple enough. Germany, ruled by a ruthless dictatorship that permitted no opposition, could put all its resources into the buildup of its armed forces. Germany's motto in those days was "Guns, not butter." By September, 1939, the Luftwaffe had more than 3,600 modern, first line airplanes, not including some 500 military transport planes.

As a democracy, Britain could not match this all-out effort. Some people in Britain strongly opposed the arms buildup. Most simply could not understand its urgency. Britain, unfortunately, was hampered by a "business as usual" attitude in those days. By September, 1939, the Royal Air Force had, for home defense, less than 1,500 planes. Yet even this does not give a true picture of the situation. Britain's force of fighter planes, known as Fighter Command, numbered less than 700 aircraft. It was this force which would have to bear the brunt of the German attack during the Battle of Britain. So, in effect, approximately 660 R.A.F. fighter planes were matched against more than 3,600 Luftwaffe bombers and fighters. The odds in favor of the Germans were roughly five to one.

Given these odds, the Battle of Britain should have been a disaster for the R.A.F. In fact, the R.A.F. did come very close to defeat at one point. Yet, when all the smoke had cleared, it was the Germans who had lost and Fighter Command that had come out on top. To understand how this was possible, one has to see what the British were up to between 1934 and 1939.

When the British decided to expand the Royal Air Force in 1934, they were aware that the days of wood and canvas biplanes armed with just two machine guns were about over. Something radically different was needed to contend with bombers based less than one hour away from London.

The first answer the British came up with was two new fast metal monoplanes armed with eight machine guns each. At the Hawker factory in Kingston, the Hurricane fighter was being developed. This monoplane had a tubular metal frame covered with canvas. It was, in a sense, a compromise with the older, traditional wood and canvas aircraft. Because of its simple structure, it could be produced quickly. Also, as it turned out later, it was easy to repair. Equipped with a Rolls Royce Merlin engine, it was capable of nearly 320 miles an hour. At the Supermarine factory at Southampton, the Spitfire fighter was being developed. The Spitfire was a sleek, all-metal monoplane capable of 355 miles an hour. It, too, was powered by a Rolls Royce Merlin engine. Highly maneuverable, it was in its day the finest fighter plane anywhere. So, while in quantity the British were far behind the Germans, in quality they were second to none.

What was the theory behind arming these planes with eight machine guns? It was thought that because of the high speed of future air combat, fighter planes would not be able to hold a bomber in their gun sights for more than two seconds at a time. A ballistics officer showed that it would take at least eight machine guns firing at the rate of a thousand rounds a minute each to destroy a bomber in two seconds. As a result, the Hurricanes and Spitfires were equipped with eight rapid-firing American Browning machine guns. Each gun had about 300 rounds of ammunition, or enough to fire for about 15 seconds.

It was the Hurricanes and Spitfires with their eight-gun armament that would save Britain in the summer of 1940. Yet their production was painfully slow at first. (There were, of course, various "bugs" that had to be eliminated before production could begin.) The first production Hurricane did not come off the assembly line until October, 1937. The first Spitfires did not reach the R.A.F. until

17

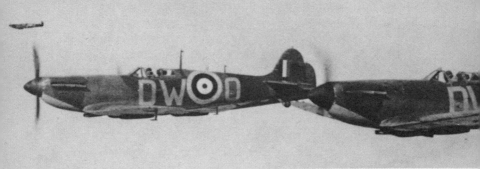

They saved Britain: the Hurricane, *top*; Spitfire, *below*.

August, 1938, when they still had to be fitted with guns and
otherwise made serviceable. At the time of the Munich crisis in September, 1938, when Britain *almost* went to war
with Germany, Fighter Command had fewer than 100 Hurricanes in service and no Spitfires at all. The interlude between the Munich agreement and the outbreak of war in
September, 1939, greatly benefited the R.A.F. By then, the
R.A.F. had 18 Hurricane squadrons and nine Spitfire squadrons in service, making a total of about 432 of these planes.
When the Battle of Britain began in July, 1940, Fighter
Command was equipped preponderantly with Hurricanes
and Spitfires.

The development of fast monoplane fighters with eight
machine guns was one answer to the problem of contending

18

German bomb crew readies Heinkel 111 for raid on Britain.

with enemy bombers. Yet there were many people who believed that the bomber would "always be able to get through" to its target, regardless of fighters. Their reasoning was this:

The enemy bomber held the initiative. It had the choice of when and where to strike. Large parts of England could be reached within 20 minutes by enemy bombers based on the continent. How could the fighter plane, which took ten minutes or more to get off the ground and reach operational altitude, be able to intercept the bomber in time? Fighter patrols *could* be maintained in the air constantly, but it would require a huge number of planes to patrol every area that needed protection.

Many suggestions were made to cope with the problem

of enemy bombers. One idea, widely accepted, was that the best defense was an offense. Britain's best hope, it was said, lay in building up a large force of bombers that could cripple the enemy on his own soil. As a result, the R.A.F. built twice as many bomber squadrons as fighter squadrons until the war began.

Other suggestions were made, some of them pure science fiction. Yet, from one of these "oddball" suggestions came an idea that was to revolutionize air defense and, during the Battle of Britain, help the R.A.F. enormously. This suggestion, made in 1934, was that British scientists should try to develop a "death ray" that would destroy enemy bombers. A committee of scientists had already been formed in Britain to study new means of coping with the bomber. Without much enthusiasm, the committee decided to look into the "death ray" idea, long a favorite of comic-strip writers. The committee soon came to the conclusion that there was little chance of crippling enemy bombers or their crews by electromagnetic radiation — so called "death rays." But, it decided, there was some possibility of *detecting* enemy aircraft from a distance by means of radio. (Sound-locator devices, used in World War I to detect enemy bombers, would be useless against the high speed bombers of the future.) The committee then asked Mr. Robert Watson-Watt, a physicist who had worked for years on high frequency radio research, to look into the matter. Watson-Watt also concluded that the idea of destruction by radio was impractical. But, he said, radio detection could work. His idea basically was that the metal parts of airplanes reflected radio pulses, and that these pulses could be recorded. Watson-Watt was then asked to give a practical demonstration of his idea.

Robert Watson-Watt, inventor of radar, at work in 1941.

The demonstration took place on February 26, 1935. An R.A.F. bomber was flown back and forth between the towns of Daventry and Wolverton. In a field at Weedon, over which the plane passed three times, its progress was being watched in a rather novel way. Watson-Watt and other scientists were gathered around a wireless receiving set to which was attached a cathode-ray oscillograph. The men saw the radiation from Daventry as a straight line on the oscillograph. But when the R.A.F. bomber flew overhead, the line vibrated back and forth more than an inch. In the words of Denis Richards, the R.A.F. historian, "It had been demonstrated beyond doubt that electromagnetic energy was reflected from an aircraft, and that these reflec-

21

tions could be depicted visually by the cathode-ray apparatus."

The significance of this demonstration was enormous. Eventually it would mean that enemy bombers would not be able to sneak over Britain's coastline undetected. British fighters, given early warning of their approach, would have precious minutes to get into the air and intercept the bombers. And it gave the R.A.F. another great advantage: The fighters would not have to maintain constant patrols, spreading themselves out thin. In effect, the new apparatus would increase the strength of Fighter Command many times.

The importance of this new apparatus was not lost on the little group of British scientists who watched the demonstration that day. Watson-Watt remarked, "England has become an island once more." At first the apparatus was referred to as R.D.F., short for radio direction-finding. Later, of course, it was simply called radar, an American term. Radar would play a tremendous part in the Battle of Britain, as the Luftwaffe would discover to its dismay.

It would be a long time before the primitive apparatus demonstrated at Weedon could be developed into an effective radar screen that would help shield Britain from attack. But work on it went ahead full speed. When the war broke out, Britain had a chain of 20 radar stations that could detect enemy planes at a distance of 100 miles or more. They could even sort out hostile planes from friendly ones. The information from these radar stations could be swiftly transmitted to Fighter Command airfields. Britain's fighter pilots, alerted by loudspeakers shouting "Scramble, squadron, scramble!" would be ready to meet the attackers.

Scramble! Fighter pilots race to get planes in the air.

CHAPTER III
BRITAIN
STANDS ALONE

World War II began on September 1, 1939, when German planes, tanks, and motorized troops invaded Poland with overwhelming force and without a formal declaration of war. Poland's Air Force of 400 planes was destroyed on the ground within two days. Most Polish resistance was crushed within a few days more, although Warsaw managed to hold out until September 27. (As a consequence, the Polish capital was subjected to heavy terror-bombing attacks from the air.) This was a new kind of warfare, which the Germans called *blitzkrieg*, or lightning war. It depended for its success on speed, mobility, and sudden death from the skies. The Luftwaffe did its job well. Stuka dive-bombers, the Junkers 87's, attacked Polish troops while other bombers blasted airfields, bridges, and railroads. Polish cities were also heavily assaulted by bombers.

Great Britain and France, pledged to support Poland against attack, declared war on Germany on September 3. There was little they could do to help Poland, however. Russian armies invaded Poland from the east on September 17 and, one day after Warsaw surrendered to the Germans, the country was dismembered. (Russia and Germany had signed a "nonaggression" pact on August 23, 1939, which, in effect, made them partners.)

For the next six months, the German High Command held its war machine in check. The German army spent the

Ju 87's, the feared *Stuka* dive-bombers, attack Poland.

The top of a Maginot Line fort, shortly after war began.

winter comfortably behind its Siegfried Line of defenses, while the French army did the same behind its Maginot Line. The Maginot Line was a chain of concrete and steel underground forts that the French built in the 1930's to protect their eastern border facing Germany. It extended from Switzerland to Luxembourg, but did not cover the border with Belgium. The Maginot Line gave the French a sense of security during the 1930's. They believed that no enemy would be able to penetrate it. When the Germans launched their offensive against France in May, 1940, this security turned out to be illusory. The Germans simply bypassed the Maginot Line and struck through Belgium. Two days after the fall of Paris, they easily broke through the Maginot defenses at two places.

The Siegfried Line, built by the Germans along their French frontier, faced the Maginot Line and was quite similar in construction. However, the Germans relied on a

German troops use pontoon bridge in invasion of Holland.

mobile attack to defeat their enemies in World War II, rather than a fixed line of defenses. (The American First Army penetrated the Siegfried Line with some difficulty in 1944.)

So here were the Germans and the French, each sitting behind their lines and pelting each other with little more than propaganda leaflets. U.S. newspapers began calling World War II the "phony war." In Britain, a listless population called it the "Bore War," a reference to the earlier, unpopular Boer War.

But, with the end of winter, the Germans struck again. On April 9, they invaded Norway and Denmark. Denmark succumbed almost immediately. Britain sent some troops to aid Norway, but they were not enough to prevent a swift German conquest of the country.

The ease with which the Germans subdued Denmark and Norway shocked the British people and caused a political

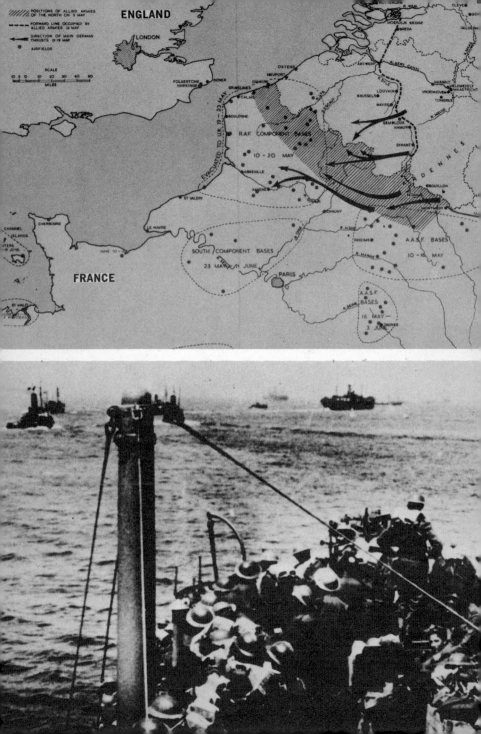

POSITIONS OF ALLIED ARMIES
OF THE NORTH ON 9 MAY
FORWARD LINE OCCUPIED BY
ALLIED ARMIES 12 MAY
DIRECTION OF MAIN GERMAN
THRUSTS 13-19 MAY
AIRFIELDS

SCALE

MILES

ENGLAND

LONDON

FRANCE

crisis at home. After a stormy debate in Parliament, Prime Minister Neville Chamberlain, who had been associated with a prewar policy of "appeasing" Germany, resigned on May 10. The reins of government were taken over by Winston Churchill, who had long warned against the threat of Nazi Germany. Churchill told the British people three days later that he had nothing to offer them but "blood, toil, tears, and sweat." He was not exaggerating the seriousness of the situation. On the very same day that he became Prime Minister, May 10, German armies opened a powerful onslaught against Holland and Belgium, with whom Germany was not even at war, and France.

Employing the same blitzkrieg tactics that had been so successful in Poland, the Germans overwhelmed Holland in five days, and Belgium in 17. Within a few days, too, the French armies began to crumble under the pressure of the German blows. One German column, pushing westward, soon reached the Channel coast, trapping the bulk of the British army and other Allied troops above it. The entrapped forces began to fall back toward Dunkirk on the coast. Escape by sea was the only possibility. From May 26 to June 4, nearly 340,000 of these troops, mostly British, were taken aboard British Navy destroyers, transports, and some small craft, and removed to England. Carried out despite constant air and artillery bombardment, the successful retreat from the beaches of Dunkirk temporarily heartened the British people.

Meanwhile, other German armies were pushing on relentlessly through France. On June 14, they entered Paris, and a week later France surrendered. It had taken the German armies just five weeks to overrun western Europe.

Left, top: Map shows German army attacks in May, 1940. **Below:** British troops are brought home from Dunkirk.

Britain now stood alone, assisted only by token forces from its overseas dominions, against the all-powerful German war machine. From the Channel coast, German officers, peering through high-power binoculars, could clearly see the cliffs of Dover, England, just 20 miles away. The tiger was separated from its prey by a narrow moat, the English Channel, that had frustrated other would-be conquerors for hundreds of years. To the Germans, who had swept all before them, it did not now look very imposing.

At this point let us see what was happening in Britain while Germany was overrunning western Europe in May and June. There was, as noted, a good deal of apathy among the British people toward the war while it was in its "phony" stage. There was also, especially in London, a considerable amount of "griping" about the nightly blackouts that were causing so many traffic accidents and fatalities. Among the lower classes was a strong feeling of alienation. Britain had just been through a long depression, and there had been much unemployment and suffering. Many working class people asked, "Why should *we* fight *their* war?" *They*, of course, were the middle and upper classes. Pacifism, nourished by Britain's huge losses in World War I, had taken a strong hold on many people. British Fascists and Communists, though a small minority, were outspoken opponents of the war effort now that Hitler and Stalin, the Russian dictator, were partners for the moment. But perhaps even more important, there was a feeling on the part of most people that Britain could not win the war under the leadership of Neville Chamberlain.

This attitude of apathy began to change when the Germans started conquering western Europe. For the first time the British people understood what a formidable foe they were up against; they realized also how close they were to invasion and conquest themselves. With France defeated, it was obvious to all that Britain would be next on Hitler's list.

Inspired by a new Prime Minister, Winston Churchill, whose speeches carried both a warning of what was to come and a calm reassurance that Britain would somehow prevail, the British people put aside apathy and class differences and turned to the difficult task of defending their island.

On May 14, 1940, Anthony Eden, Britain's Secretary of State for War, broadcast an appeal for the formation of a volunteer force of male civilians to help guard Britain against the threat of German parachute invaders. Even before he had finished speaking, thousands of men between the ages of 16 and 65 had rushed to local police stations to volunteer. Within six days, more than a quarter of a million had enrolled and, by August, this new citizens' army, later called the Home Guard, numbered more than a million. Despite its enthusiasm, the Home Guard was not at first a very formidable force. Britain was at this time shockingly bereft of arms with which to defend itself. The British Expeditionary Force had been forced to leave almost all its weapons behind at Dunkirk. At home, the arsenal was bare. "Never," said Winston Churchill later, "has a great nation been so naked before her foes." About one third of the volunteers were armed with rifles. The rest had such weapons as shotguns, sporting rifles, golf clubs, axes, pikes, and sticks. (It was called the "broomstick army" by its critics.) Such a force would hardly have been a match for German parachutists armed with submachine guns and grenades.

Yet the Home Guard did a valuable job even then of supplementing the regular army. With great vigor, it went about its job of patrolling and standing guard at bridges, factories, and government offices, and zealously watching some 5,000 miles of coastline. It built up roadblocks,

31

trudged the fields (or sometimes rode them on horseback), and even manned motor boats on large lakes. Simply by relieving the regular Army of such duties, the Home Guard played an important role in the defense of the island. Later, when rifles and other arms began arriving from the United States, the Home Guard became a well-trained, well-armed force.

While the early Home Guard was patrolling the fields with shotguns and golf clubs, the regular Army was in a pitiful state. Most of the British Expeditionary Force had been rescued from the disaster in France, but what would it use for weapons? Britain's Home Defense forces, those who had remained stationed in the British isles, were better off, but only relatively so. Some idea of the weakness of Home Defense at this time, May and June of 1940, may be gathered from the condition of the First London Division, assigned to guard a vital section of the southeast coast against enemy invasion. Its armament was as follows: 23 field guns, instead of the 72 it was supposed to have, no tanks, no armored cars, no medium machine guns, no antitank guns, and about one sixth of the antitank rifles it needed. Even so, the First London Division was better armed than other Home Defense divisions. Some British regulars did not even have rifles.

In May, Winston Churchill, foreseeing the possibility of France's defeat, asked the British Chiefs of Staff to give him an estimate of Britain's ability to carry on the war alone. Their answer, as reported by Basil Collier in his book, *The Defence of the United Kingdom*, was that it was impossible "to say whether or not the United Kingdom could hold out in all circumstances." They felt that whether the enemy's attempt to enforce surrender took the form of blockade, invasion, or "a knockout blow," his opening move would probably be air attack. If the air defenses proved effective,

Left, top: Defense volunteers getting rifles in May, 1940. **Below:** Better-armed Home Guards five months later.

and if the gravity of the threat was brought home to the people, Britain should stand a good chance of survival. *"The crux of the whole problem,"* said the Chiefs of Staff, *"is the air defense of this country."*

As if to emphasize the point, they said that because of Britain's shortage of destroyers and other patrol vessels, and her long coastline, it would be impossible for the Navy to keep out all seaborne invaders, *especially if the enemy had air superiority.* But, they were asked, if the enemy could not be kept out, what were the chances of defeating him once he had gained a foothold on the British coast? Their answer was grim:

"Should the Germans succeed in establishing a force with its vehicles in this country, our army forces have not got the offensive power to drive it out."

So everything at this point depended upon the ability of the Royal Air Force to repel an invasion and safeguard Britain until its defenses could be built up.

What was the condition of the R.A.F., and especially Fighter Command, at this time? Not very good. The R.A.F. had been badly pummeled during the fighting in France. When the Germans began their offensive on May 10, the British had about 400 planes in France. Of these, about 100 were fighters. The rest were chiefly light bombers. The main French air arm numbered about 450 planes, most of which were quite obsolete. These 850 British and French planes of all types were opposing a German Luftwaffe made up of about 3,820 modern aircraft. It was, of course, no contest. The Luftwaffe destroyed the French Air Force within a few days. The R.A.F. gave a better account of itself, but it, too, was hard hit. British light bombers, mainly Battles and Blenheims, took very heavy losses. On one day, May 14, 40 of 71 of these bombers were destroyed in action. As for the fighters, mainly Hurricanes, they had considerable success in combat; but, fighting against such heavy odds, they too were gradually being chewed up. Great pressure was put on Churchill by France's Premier, Paul Reynaud, to send more fighter squadrons to France. At first, Churchill complied, sending a few at a time. But this was like tossing them piecemeal into a meat grinder. In Britain, Air Chief Marshal Hugh Dowding, head of Fighter Command, was extremely worried about the depletion of his force. He had always insisted that Britain needed at least 52 fighter squadrons at home for the defense of the island. He was already down to 43 squadrons, and now Reynaud was demanding that 10 more be sent to France.

At this point, Dowding put his foot down. Speaking before the Cabinet, he told the ministers that if the loss of fighter planes in France continued at the current rate, there would be no more Fighter Command by the end of July. The Cabinet was won over temporarily and the 10 squadrons were not sent to France. Taking no chances, Dowding then wrote a now historic letter to the chief of the Air Staff stating just how bad Fighter Command's situation was:

"I must point out that within the last few days the equivalent of 10 [fighter] squadrons have been sent to France, that the Hurricane squadrons remaining in this country are seriously depleted, and that the more squadrons which are sent to France the higher will be the wastage and the more insistent the demands for reinforcements.

"I must therefore request that as a matter of paramount urgency the Air Ministry will consider and decide what level of strength is to be left to the Fighter Command for the defense of this country, and will assure me that when this level has been reached, not one fighter will be sent across the Channel however urgent and insistent the appeals for help may be.

"I believe that if an adequate fighter force is kept in this

Air Chief Marshal Sir Hugh Dowding of Fighter Command.

country, if the Fleet remains in being, and if Home Forces are suitably organized to resist invasion, we should be able to carry on the war single-handed for some time, if not indefinitely. But if the Home Defense Force is drained away in desperate attempts to remedy the situation in France, defeat in France will involve the final, complete, and irremediable defeat of this country."

Despite Dowding's urgent pleas, Churchill felt that a last, desperate attempt had to be made to save France from collapse. Additional fighter squadrons were sent to France until Dowding was left with only 37 at home. Finally, on May 19, with the Germans rapidly overrunning French air bases, Churchill decided that no more fighter squadrons could be transferred to the continent. This decision angered France's leaders, but it was one that Churchill had to make if Britain were to be able to defend itself. Soon afterward, Britain began withdrawing its fighter squadrons from France, leaving only enough to cover the retreat from Dunkirk. Fighter

The German conquerors entering Paris in June, 1940.

squadrons operating from bases in England also aided the British army at Dunkirk, though many army men complained about their insufficient air cover.

Altogether, in the period from May 10 to June 20, Fighter Command lost 386 Hurricanes and 67 Spitfires. The loss of fighter pilots was even more serious. On June 15, Dowding found himself with approximately 466 serviceable planes, of which only 331 were Spitfires and Hurricanes. He also counted 1,094 fighter pilots, 362 fewer than required.

On June 18, the last British fighters in France left for home. Dowding desperately began to rebuild and reorganize his battered Command. If Britain's main hope for survival lay now with its fighter defenses, it was in a very bad way. Fighter Command needed a breathing spell urgently. It was Adolf Hitler who, by putting off his decision to invade Britain for several weeks, gave the vital time Fighter Command needed to recoup its strength for the oncoming Battle of Britain.

CHAPTER IV HITLER HESITATES

What was going through the mind of the German dictator in May and June of 1940? The success of the German army in western Europe went beyond anything that Hitler had expected. He did not foresee that the offensive begun on May 10 would crush France completely. His objectives for the German army in carrying out Operation Yellow, as the offensive was called, were contained in his war Directive No. 6:

"The object of this attack is to defeat as strong sections as possible of the French Army and her ally and partner in the fighting [Britain], and at the same time to acquire as great an area of Holland, Belgium, and northern France as possible, to use as a base offering good prospects for waging aerial and sea warfare against England and to provide ample coverage for the vital district of the Ruhr." (The Ruhr was the center of Germany's coal and steel industries.)

It is quite apparent that Hitler merely expected Operation Yellow to be the first round in the war against the Allies, rather than a knockout blow to France. Yet so overwhelming was the force of the German attack that within a few days nothing could stop it from overrunning all of France. Under the circumstances, what did Hitler intend to do about Britain? Did he, or the German High Command, or anyone in Germany for that matter, have a plan for invading Britain? The answer is no. War Directive No. 6,

The Fuehrer, Adolf Hitler, looked confident in May, 1939.

Grand Admiral Erich Raeder, center, on German submarine.

which called merely for "waging aerial and sea warfare against England," indicates clearly that there was no invasion plan. A study had been made of the problems of waging war with Britain, but it dealt with broad matters of strategy, rather than with specific details.

Yet, as early as May 21, the subject of invading Britain was raised by Grand Admiral Erich Raeder, Commander-in-Chief of the German Navy. On that day, Raeder told Hitler that the German Navy had been examining the problem for some time, and wished to discuss it with the Fuehrer. Hitler showed no interest in Raeder's proposal at all. He had other fish to fry at this time — the destruction of France's armies. Raeder did not raise the subject again until June 20. By this time, France was on the verge of surrender, and Hitler was master of most of Europe. According to Peter Fleming, author of *Operation Sea Lion* (the German code name for invasion of Britain), Raeder re-

ported on "the preparations for an invasion of England . . .
the locality chosen for landing . . . mines . . . shipping . . .
special craft . . . air supremacy."

Again Hitler showed no interest. He talked to Raeder
about the possibility of settling Jews on the island of Mada-
gascar, and a plan for invading Iceland, but said nothing
about invading England. He was probably throwing away
his best chance to win the war, for at this time Britain's
army was without the means of repelling an attack, and its
Air Force was dangerously depleted. Why then did Hitler
fail to grasp the opportunity? Undoubtedly, he had strong
reservations about Germany's ability to carry out a seaborne
invasion of Britain at this time. Germany's military machine
was immensely powerful and resourceful, but it had had
very little experience in amphibious operations. And, while
the Luftwaffe had demonstrated in the Norway campaign
that naval vessels were highly vulnerable to air attack, the
British Navy still must have appeared to Hitler a formidable
force.

Beyond such military considerations, Hitler hesitated because he seriously misjudged the British people. He believed
them to be a flabby, disunited, decadent lot. When France
fell, he fully expected that the British would surrender
without a fight. Or, at the very least, he *hoped* that they
would. In this, he couldn't have been more mistaken. Once
the British people awoke to the seriousness of their situation
and at last had a Prime Minister who inspired confidence,
they could not have been more united or determined to
fight. Moreover, they were confident they would prevail. In
the summer of 1940, when many political and military leaders in the United States were predicting Britain's downfall,
the British people were exhibiting a cheerful self-
confidence, exemplified by signs appearing in windows ev-
erywhere saying, in typical British fashion, "We are not in-

Churchill visits troops guarding coast, August, 1940.

terested in the possibilities of defeat. They do not exist."
Prime Minister Winston Churchill, who inspired and re-
flected this spirit, summed it up with simple eloquence on
June 4, 1940. On that day, when the last British soldiers
were being brought home from Dunkirk, Churchill told the
House of Commons:

"We shall not flag or fail. . . . We shall defend our island
whatever the cost may be. We shall fight on the beaches.
We shall fight on the landing grounds. We shall fight in the
fields and in the streets. We shall fight in the hills. *We shall
never surrender.*"

While Hitler hesitated, the British people rolled up their
sleeves and went to work. Weeks of hectic activity followed
as Britain steeled itself against invasion. War production
began to climb steadily. In the factories, men worked long
hours until, exhausted, they fell asleep at their machines. In
homes, middle-aged women held "filing parties" after tea to

A British soldier guards coast defense guns in 1940.

smooth down the rough edges of machine parts. In school workshops, boys helped rim the edges of airplane seats with hammers that were too big for some of them to hold. At Navy and civilian dockyards, work was rushed on repairing Britain's destroyer fleet, which had been battered at Dunkirk. In ports and harbors, obstacles were built to prevent invasion ships from entering. The Army drilled in the techniques of mobile warfare as it waited for its new equipment. At the same time, it built up coastal defenses with new six-inch guns, mines, barbed wire entanglements, and concealed pillboxes.

The Royal Air Force was busiest of all. By the middle of July, six new radar stations had been added to Britain's chain. A new Fighter Command group was formed and new airfields built. The Royal Observer Corps, a volunteer group whose members scanned the skies with binoculars for enemy planes, was strengthened. Balloons were added to those which already hung over Britain's cities and ports, serving as a deterrent to low-flying enemy planes. A number of new antiaircraft guns were produced, although these were still in very short supply.

Fighter Command was strengthened by the creation of a new Ministry of Aircraft Production under Lord Beaverbrook. A tireless taskmaster, Beaverbrook drove the aircraft industry hard, and he got results. By the middle of July, fighter plane losses suffered in France had been made good. The British were still short of all weapons, but the situation was much better than it had been in May and June, and was improving daily.

Despite feverish activity on the part of Britain's Army and Navy, no one doubted that it was the Royal Air Force which would first bear the full brunt of the German attack, when it came. On June 18, Churchill told the House of Commons:

"I look forward confidently to the exploits of our fighter pilots — these splendid men, this brilliant youth — who will have the glory of saving their native land, their island home, and all they love, from the most deadly of all attacks."

The fate of Britain, perhaps of the world, was in the hands of about 1,000 young men, some of them professionals, but most of them drawn from the Volunteer Reserve — the amateur "weekend pilots." Their average age was 20 and they had at their disposal fewer than 700 planes. Almost all of them affected a devil-may-care attitude that later became a cover-up for the terrible tensions and pressures of battle.

Al "Sailor" Malan, possibly Britain's greatest ace. A South African, he later aided black rights movement.

CHAPTER V
THE AIR BATTLE
BEGINS
(JULY 10–AUGUST 12, 1940)

During the month of June, while Hitler was turning his back on the problem of invading England, the German Luftwaffe was beginning to carry out small, scattered raids on the island, mostly by night. On the night of June 5, about 30 German planes attacked airfields and other targets near the east coast of England. On the next night, there were similar raids. From then until the fall of France, about June 20, there was a lull. The attacks then resumed on an almost nightly basis. For the most part, they did little damage, although air raid warnings caused many in Britain to lose sleep. The Germans suffered few losses in planes.

The object of these flights, apart from giving German bomber crews experience in night flying over Britain, was to test a German navigational and bombing aid known as *Knickebein* (crooked leg). Basically, Knickebein was a system of radio beams transmitted from Germany. If the German pilot was flying on course, he heard a steady note in his earphone. If he was deviating from his course, he heard a series of dots and dashes that warned him accordingly. When the pilot approached his target, the beam was intersected by another radio beam, which caused a different note to sound in his ear phone. At this point, the pilot released his bombs. Knickebein was a secret weapon, and, if it could have been perfected, it would have been an invaluable aid to the Luftwaffe in carrying out bombing raids, especially at night.

Hitler and Field Marshal Keitel study map, June, 1940.

Unfortunately for the Luftwaffe, a British physicist, Dr. R. V. Jones, attached to the intelligence branch of the Air Ministry, began to suspect what the Germans were up to. He was soon able to confirm his suspicions and, before long, a unit was formed to counteract Knickebein. By August, this unit was able to devise a way of "jamming" the German radio beams using high-powered hospital X-ray equipment. This simply made it impossible for the German pilot to hear his Knickebein beams. Such "jamming" methods wrecked the Knickebein system and helped prevent accurate night bombing by the Luftwaffe when the Battle of Britain entered that phase. At the end of June, the score stood thus:

The Luftwaffe had gained some experience in night flying and had caused some discomfort and a few casualties in Britain. The British had gained some experience in air raid alerts while downing about 11 Luftwaffe planes. More important, they had discovered an important "secret weapon" and were learning how to deal with it.

While these raids were taking place at the end of June, what was Adolf Hitler doing? After the fall of France, he spent about 10 days at a country retreat in Germany's Black Forest. During that time, he was largely out of touch with the German High Command. This was hardly the behavior of a man bent on bringing the war to a swift conclusion. Finally, on July 2, Hitler stirred himself to action. On that day, Field Marshal Wilhelm Keitel issued a directive in the name of Hitler that set in motion the machinery for invading Britain:

"The Fuehrer and Supreme Commander has decided that a landing in England is possible, *provided that air superiority can be attained*, and certain other conditions fulfilled."

This order well reflected Hitler's indecision about invading Britain. It did not actually order an invasion, nor did it set a date. It merely said that an invasion was "possible."

Preparations were to begin at once, but were "to be undertaken on the basis that the invasion is still only a plan, and has not been decided on."

The key words in this order were, of course, "provided that air superiority can be attained. . . ." In so wording the order, Hitler had placed the burden of making an invasion possible squarely upon the German Luftwaffe.

What kind of force was the Luftwaffe? It was literally the most powerful air force in the world, and it was supremely confident. After all, it had never suffered a defeat. It had easily crushed the air forces of Poland, Norway, and France, and had inflicted heavy losses on the R.A.F. in the skies over France. And yet the Luftwaffe had never been thoroughly tested in combat. It was no great feat to overcome the small, largely obsolete air forces of its early victims. And the R.A.F. force in France, small and heavily outnumbered, had given a good account of itself. None of this seemed to bother the Luftwaffe in June, 1940. It had conquered all, and England, with its many large industrial centers, was now only a few minutes away from the Channel coast. It must have seemed a very easy target.

Here the Luftwaffe oversimplified. It had been created mainly as a *tactical* air force, designed to give the German army close support on the battlefield. It was thought of as "flying artillery" by the German High Command. The Luftwaffe was *not* designed to carry out strategic bombing —the devastation of industrial and communications centers behind the enemy lines. The Germans did not have a force of large, four-engined bombers capable of carrying heavy bomb loads long distances. Its bomber force consisted almost entirely of twin-engined medium bombers whose "payload" was relatively limited. They could not inflict the kind of damage that in later years four-engined U.S. and British bombers inflicted on German cities.

As for the Luftwaffe's fighter planes, they, too, had problems that would become apparent in the Battle of Britain. The Messerschmitt 109, Germany's best fighter at the time, was faster than the Hurricane and almost as fast as the Spitfire. It could outclimb or outdive both, but was less maneuverable in turning. It was an excellent plane, well-armed with two machine guns and two 20 mm. cannon. However, its range was short. Once over England, the Me 109 pilot did not have enough fuel left for prolonged combat. The Me 110, a twin-engined fighter-bomber with a crew of two, had greater range, but it was no match for the Spitfire in either speed or maneuverability.

Apart from such deficiencies, the Luftwaffe was handicapped by the almost complete absence of radar and a radio ground control system. These glaring weaknesses were largely due to Reichsmarshal Hermann Goering, who was quite unable to understand or appreciate the capabilities of advanced technology. This inability would cost him dearly during the Battle of Britain, when British radar and radio ground control would play such decisive roles.

Yet, as the Battle of Britain began to unfold, the Luftwaffe was undoubtedly a formidable force. It was modern, efficient, and its pilots were first-rate. For the attack against England, the Luftwaffe mustered about 3,500 planes, of which some 2,600 were serviceable. About 1,200 were medium, twin-engined bombers, chiefly Dornier 17's, Heinkel 111's, and Junkers 88's. About 320 were Junkers 87's, the Stuka dive-bombers. Some 800 were single-engined fighters, the Me 109's. About 250 were twin-engined fighter-bombers, the Me 110's.

These planes were divided among three *Luftflotten* (Air

Right, top: **The Me 109, Germany's best fighter plane in Battle of Britain.** *Below:* **The Junkers 88, a fast bomber.**

Fleets), numbered 2, 3, and 5. Luftflotte 2, commanded by Field Marshal Albert Kesselring, was based in Holland, Belgium, and northeast France. Luftflotte 3, commanded by Field Marshal Hugo Sperrle, was based in northwest France. Luftflotte 5, the smallest of the three air fleets, was based in Norway and Denmark and was commanded by General Hans-Juergen Stumpff. A vertical line was drawn by the Luftwaffe command that split England roughly in two. Luftflotte 2 would attack targets east of the line. Luftflotte 3 would attack targets west of the line. Luftflotte 5 would make diversionary attacks on northeast England and southeast Scotland.

Opposing this enormous force was the R.A.F.'s Fighter Command, headed by Air Chief Marshal Sir Hugh Dowding. On July 10, when the Battle of Britain began, Dowding had approximately 660 planes. They were divided into four Groups. No. 11 Group, commanded by Air Vice-Marshal Keith Park, defended southeast England, including the city of London. This group, which bore the brunt of the battle, had 22 squadrons. No. 10 Group, commanded by Air Vice-Marshal Sir Quintin Brand, defended southwest England, and had four squadrons. No. 12 Group, commanded by Air Vice-Marshal T. L. Leigh-Mallory, defended the English midlands, and had 14 squadrons. No 13 Group, commanded by Air Vice-Marshal R. E. Saul, defended the north and had 14 squadrons.

How did Fighter Command's defense system work? Information on enemy raids was picked up by radar stations before the German formations reached the English coast. After they had passed the coast (where the radar stations were located), their movements were followed by members

Left, top: The Me 110, a fighter-bomber. *Center:* The Dornier 17 bomber. *Bottom:* The Heinkel 111 bomber.

Left: Map shows Fighter Command's defenses in August, 1940.
Above: A Fighter Command operations room in action.

of the Royal Observer Corps. Information was relayed simultaneously to operations rooms at Fighter Command Headquarters, Group Headquarters, and to sector stations. (Each group was subdivided into sectors which controlled two or three airfields. A sector station was located on or next to an airfield.) The operations rooms, or "ops" as they were usually called, were the nerve centers of the defense system. An operations room looked like this:

In the center of the room was a huge table on which was a map outlining England, the English Channel, and a large part of northern France. Around the map stood members of the Women's Auxiliary Air Force, equipped with headphones and holding long sticks. These women were known as "plotters." As they received information about enemy flights, they indicated these on the map with markers which they moved around with their sticks. Looking down on the map from above were the controllers. They could see in a moment exactly what was happening and issue the necessary orders to fighter squadrons to intercept. The job of the Group controller was to decide which of his sectors would deal with a raid, how many planes should be sent up, and which squadrons to use. The sector controllers passed these orders on to the squadrons and, once they were in the air, directed them to enemy formations. They also guided the planes back to the airfields after they had broken off action.

Hitler's directive of July 2, calling for air superiority as a first step toward an invasion of Britain, soon stirred the Luftwaffe to sharp activity. By July 10, it was busy enough to stretch Dowding's forces quite thin. For this reason, the British generally mark the beginning of the Battle of Britain on this day. From July 10 until August 12, the Luftwaffe concentrated on attacking ship convoys passing through the English Channel as well as English ports on the Channel. Its main objective was to wear down Fighter Command, but in this it was quite unsuccessful. During this period, the first phase of the Battle of Britain, Fighter Command lost 148 planes, much less than one month's production of fighter aircraft. The Luftwaffe lost 286 planes. While losing almost twice as many planes as Fighter Command, the Luftwaffe had been able to inflict only minor losses on British shipping.

What was the fighting on July 10 like? The first half of the day passed with relatively light activity. But around 1:30 in the afternoon, radar stations in southeast England spotted a large German formation shaping up behind Calais on the French coast. Its objective was a ship convoy off Dover, England, that was being guarded by six Hurricanes. The German formation numbered about 20 bombers es-

Bombs falling on Portland, England, on the Channel coast.

corted by about 40 single-engined and twin-engined fighters. A lively half-hour action followed, in which the six Hurricanes were joined by elements of other fighter squadrons. The fight cost the Luftwaffe four fighter planes. Three Hurricanes were lost, and one small ship was sunk.

This action, the first large engagement of the Battle of Britain, established a pattern for future air combat in the struggle:

1. British radar was able to spot the oncoming German formation and give warning — about 20 minutes — to Fighter Command.

2. Throughout the engagement, the Germans outnumbered the British.

3. Despite being outnumbered, the British suffered fewer losses than the Germans.

There were several reasons why the British were generally outnumbered even though they had the advantage of early warning by radar. In the beginning, at least, British radar operators were not able to gauge accurately the size (or height) of enemy formations from the "blips" that appeared on their screens. Often they underestimated the number of German planes. Operations room controllers tended to be cautious. How did they know that the blip on the radar screen was a real attack or merely a feint by the Germans? Suppose it were just a feint — then they must keep enough fighters to deal with the real attack later on. As a result, often only a half-dozen fighters were sent to intercept German formations that might number at least 30 planes. There was another reason why British fighter planes were usually so outnumbered. It took a Hurricane about 16 minutes to climb to 20,000 feet. A Spitfire reached that altitude in 13 minutes. It took the German formations, on the average, about 20 minutes to cross the Channel and reach their targets. That gave the fighters only a few minutes to

Alan Deere at the time of the Battle of Britain, 1940.

intercept the enemy formations at operational altitude. To
assemble three or four fighter squadrons in the air at once
took time. The German formations might easily reach their
targets before the fighters could be grouped in a large
"wing." As a result, fighter squadrons were usually sent up
one or two at a time. That the British pilots did so well in
spite of the odds against them was a tribute to their ability
and the quality of the planes they flew.

How did a British Spitfire pilot feel when he found himself heavily outnumbered by the enemy? Flight Lieutenant
Alan Deere, now an Air Commodore with the R.A.F., recalled it this way in the French aviation magazine, *Icare*:

"On sighting an overwhelmingly large enemy formation
there was a sort of hysterical humor at the hopelessness of
the task, erased almost immediately by the onset of quick,
stabbing shafts of fear as the armada of aircraft drew closer,
and finally, before joining combat, a consciousness of a

59

thudding and moist brow accompanied by a breathless, panicky fear."

Deere remembers well his first "kill" in combat, the exact date not certain, but about July 10. This is the way he describes it:

"My flight was ordered off to intercept, in the words of the controller, '50+ enemy aircraft approaching from the east at 17,000 feet.' And they *were* at this height, and there were at least 50 — Heinkel 111's escorted by Me 109's. [It was] a black-spotted mass, which forged its way across the sky intent on its target — a convoy of some 20 merchant ships which puffed and smoked a passage through the troubled English Channel . . . 'Tally-ho, Red Leader,' the sighting report came excitedly over the Radio Telephone from my number two [plane].

" 'Yes, I've seen them,' I replied. 'We'll climb up behind the fighters and try and draw them off.' So I issued my orders to my flight of six planes against 50+. We were to become accustomed to such odds.

"But the enemy fighter escort was not to be drawn off. Indeed, it was we who were diverted from our task of getting at the bombers by a frontal assault from a small detachment of 109's which had broken formation to ward off the interfering Spitfires.

" 'Attack individually,' I ordered. I barely had time to issue the order before the 109's were among us. Experience over Dunkirk had taught me that when attacked the best counter was to go into a right turn. In this maneuver, the Spitfire was infinitely superior to the Me 109 and so long as one remained in the turn the enemy pilot could not bring his guns to bear. And this I did, as the German pilot flashed past, turning as he did so, to get behind me. But it was I who finished astern of him.

"The rest was easy. He could not escape the lethal cone

of fire of my eight Browning guns which poured incendiary and armor-piercing bullets into the Messerschmitt's smoky-gray hide. For a time it seemed to absorb them without apparent damage, but then a small, yellow flame began to appear from behind the cockpit. Black smoke spouted from the engine and then, as if a time bomb had been ignited, the fighter exploded in a shower of hot, flaming metal which I avoided by breaking up and away. . . . My first victory in the Battle of Britain hurtled towards its grave on English soil, its pilot undoubtedly dead in the cockpit."

Were British fighter pilots cold-hearted "killers"? Hardly, but neither were they likely to be conscience-stricken about shooting down enemy planes. Wing Commander Robert Stanford-Tuck, now retired, explained his attitude this way:

"My conscience never really pricked me in that direction. I never thought of the person inside the enemy aircraft unless I happened to see him bail out, or fall out, at the last moment. To me, it was an aircraft that, if I didn't knock it down, was going to knock me down. And it was my enemy. This was what I call the professional attitude. You had to be very cold about it. If you saw one of your own chaps go down a few thousand feet on your left, you'd think very intimately how you were with him the night before, you had breakfast with him and you knew him very well, he was a very nice young boy. But you couldn't dwell on it very long because if you did you formed a morbid outlook that just wouldn't work for a professional fighter pilot. You couldn't do it.

"As for the enemy, there certainly was never any personal animosity that I felt toward the pilot in that aircraft. It was only what the aircraft could do, how it would affect us battlewise. Many chaps I know worked themselves into a

Left: Robert Stanford-Tuck in 1940. *Above:* Stanford-Tuck and Air Marshal Sir Dermot Boyle in a recent photo.

sort of hate aspect, but I couldn't quite see the object of that because if you do that, you are losing a certain amount of your calculation. You have to be so calculating when you are up there in a high altitude with a brilliant sun. A lot of people don't understand it, but blue sky gets darker as you go up and it's a very strange cat and mouse world up there with a few little twinkling specks that you see and you know its a formation of Messerschmitts coming down to attack. You hear your boys call out from the stern, 'Look out, sir, they're coming down starboard!' That's all you hear and the next minute, whoooosh, you're turning away. It's a very cold business, and if there is a form of personal animosity, I think it's quite wrong."

Yet some of Britain's fighter pilots *did* hate their enemy. One of them was Group Captain Douglas Bader, who flew a

Left: Douglas Bader as a fighter pilot. **Above:** Bader, right, visits set of movie, **Battle of Britain,** in 1969.

fighter despite having two artificial legs. This is how Bader describes his attitude toward the German invaders:

"We hated those airplanes with their iron crosses and their crooked swastikas flying into our English sky and dropping bombs indiscriminately on our English towns. Fighting alongside us were Czechs, Poles, Norwegians, Danes, Dutch, Belgians, and French, those gallant allies who managed to escape from their own countries and join with us in stopping the hated Hun from dominating the whole of Europe. I think the Poles hated the most. Having survived for 600 years as a nation between the Teuton and the Slav, they were tough and ruthless. I well remember cursing some of the Poles fighting with me for following German airplanes already destroyed down to the ground instead of staying up and destroying others. Nevertheless, I understood their feelings."

CHAPTER VI
THE ATTACK OF
THE EAGLES
(AUGUST 13–AUGUST 23, 1940)

On July 16, 1940, Adolf Hitler issued his famous War Directive No. 16, calling, more or less, for an invasion of England:

"As England, in spite of the hopelessness of her military situation, has so far shown herself unwilling to come to any compromise, I have decided to begin preparations for, and if necessary carry out, an invasion of England.

"This operation is dictated by the necessity of eliminating Great Britain as a base from which the war against Germany can be fought. If necessary, the island will be occupied."

Although this directive was worded more strongly than his earlier directive of July 2, it was still less than forceful. Hitler spoke of Britain as being unwilling to make peace "so far." Clearly he still hoped that Britain might yet surrender without a fight. His distaste for an invasion of England was also made clear by his qualifying the order twice with the phrase, *"if necessary."*

Only three days later, on July 19, Hitler made a speech before the German Reichstag that appeared to be a "peace offer." He said:

"In this hour, I feel it to be my duty before my own conscience to appeal once more to reason and common sense in Great Britain. . . . I consider myself in a position to make this appeal since I am not a vanquished foe begging favors, but the victor, speaking in the name of reason. I can see no reason why this war need go on. I am grieved to think of the sacrifices it must claim."

A British fighter goes down in flames during air battle.

Hitler shed a few more crocodile tears toward the end of his speech. It was never his intention to destroy, or even to harm, the British Empire, he said. "It almost causes me pain to feel that I should have been selected by fate to deal the final blow to the structure which these men [Churchill and his colleagues] have already set to tottering."

Hitler's "olive branch" was greeted in Britain with laughter and derision. The very idea of Hitler having a conscience and claiming to be a man of reason was really very funny. It must have been fairly obvious by now even to Hitler that the British people had only contempt for him and his "peace offers." His Directive No. 16 had said that "the English air force must be eliminated to such an extent that it will be incapable of putting up any substantial opposition to invading troops." On August 1, in War Directive No. 17, Hitler showed that he was impatient with the progress so far of the Luftwaffe in seeking to gain its objective:

"I consider that the air and sea war against the English motherland must be carried out more firmly than previously. Therefore, I order the following: The German air forces must with all means in their power and as quickly as possible destroy the English air force. The attacks must . . . be directed against flying formations, their ground organizations, and their supply organizations . . . and against the aircraft production industry. . . ."

Hitler had given the Luftwaffe an unmistakable order: destroy the Royal Air Force. The Luftwaffe was confident it could do the job in two to four weeks. Goering, in fact, believed that the Luftwaffe could, by itself, knock Britain out of the war, making an invasion unnecessary. He and his top commanders began preparing for *Adlerangriff*, the Attack of the Eagles, which would begin on August 13, called *Adler Tag*, or Eagle Day.

While the Luftwaffe prepared to deal the knockout blow

to the R.A.F., German troops in France began intensive preparations for an invasion of England — dubbed "Sea Lion" — and the German Navy began rounding up barges, tugs, transports, and other vessels to form an invasion armada. Admiral Raeder, who was not enthusiastic about Sea Lion's prospects, told Hitler on July 31 that the invasion could not be launched before mid-September. Hitler accepted this view and added that everything hinged on the forthcoming air attack. If it failed, then the date for an invasion, tentatively set for September 15, would have to be put off until the following spring.

The Luftwaffe now decided that the key to destroying Fighter Command was to attack its forward airfields in England, those that lay close to the south coast. This would be its strategy from August 12, when the Luftwaffe "warmed up" for Eagle Day, until approximately August 23, when it adopted a new strategy.

The German attacks on August 12 were severe, but not as damaging as the Luftwaffe supposed. One radar station on the Isle of Wight was temporarily knocked out, and a number of airfields were heavily bombed. Though badly pitted with bomb craters, they managed to stay in action while the job of repairing them went on. (British pilots got used to landing their planes on cratered runways, zig-zagging around the holes.) The Luftwaffe was jubilant over these partial successes, though it had lost more planes during the day than the British. As it almost always did, the Luftwaffe claimed that British plane losses far exceeded their own. The British, too, were prone to exaggerate enemy losses, but they were generally more realistic than the Germans in this respect.

The Luftwaffe confidently expected that Eagle Day would bring even greater successes. It was not to be. The Luftwaffe's planning for Eagle Day was unaccountably careless. In one instance, a large formation of bombers took off at dawn without a fighter escort. Flying over the Thames estuary, it was pounced on by British fighters and suffered heavy losses. In another instance, Me 110's, flying without the bombers they were supposed to escort, ran into much more maneuverable British fighters over Portland on the Channel coast and lost five of their planes. A formation of Stuka dive-bombers, with inadequate fighter protection, was attacked by high-flying Spitfires. Five of the Stukas went down in flames.

By the end of the day, the Germans had suffered their worst setback of the air war so far, losing 45 planes, while Fighter Command lost only 13. At the same time, the Germans had been able to inflict only minor damage on Fighter Command airfields. Nevertheless, Luftwaffe pilots again gave highly exaggerated reports of British planes shot down and airfields destroyed. Goering may have suspected that these reports were one-sided. Certainly the strength of the opposition and the heavy losses suffered by some Luftwaffe units gave him something to think about.

Whatever his private doubts, Goering decided to go all out to deliver a knockout blow to Fighter Command. On the 15th of August, the Luftwaffe attacked in greater numbers than ever before, or ever again after. Altogether, the Luftwaffe made 1,786 sorties that day, about 300 more than on Eagle Day. The plan of the attack was breathtaking in its concept. For the first time, the Luftwaffe decided to use all three of its Luftflotten at once. Luftflotte 5, based in Norway and Denmark, would join Luftflotten 2 and 3, based in Holland, Belgium, and northern France. This was going to be a "nutcracker" operation that would break the R.A.F.

At about 10:45 A.M. a large German formation was spotted on British radar screens moving toward Kent, in southeast England. It consisted of nearly 40 Stuka dive-bombers

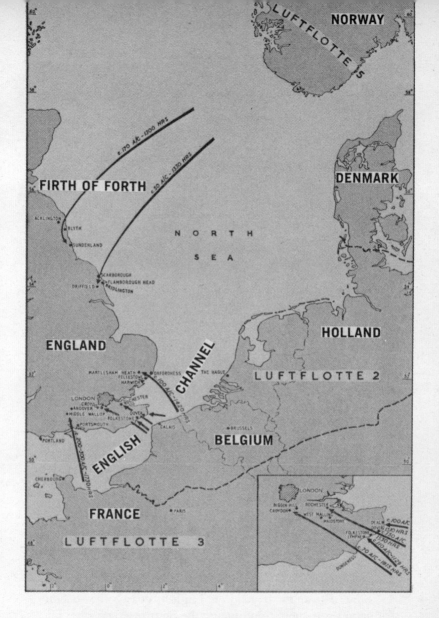

Map shows main Luftwaffe attacks on August 15, 1940.

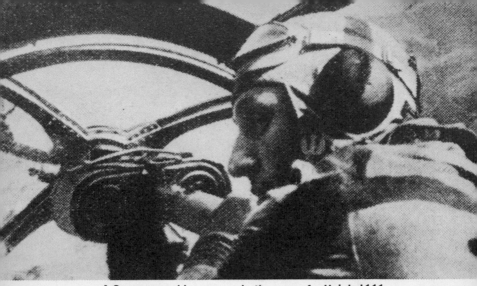

A German machine gunner in the nose of a Heinkel 111.

accompanied by about 60 single-engined fighters. Their targets were two Fighter Command airfields, Lympne and Hawkinge, near the coast. No. 11 Group ordered four fighter squadrons into the air to intercept. They were unable to prevent the bombers from heavily damaging Lympne, but Hawkinge suffered only minor damage.

The next heavy action took place much further to the north, where No. 13 Group was based. Shortly after noon, the radar chain picked up an enemy formation flying across the North Sea towards the Firth of Forth. It was estimated that the enemy force consisted of about 30 planes. Actually, it was much larger, and made up of about 65 Heinkel 111 bombers escorted by about 35 Me 110 twin-engined fighters bound from Norway. Their targets were two northern Bomber Command airfields. To meet a force believed to number 30 planes, No. 13 Group sent up two Spitfire squadrons and one Hurricane squadron, about 36 planes.

About 30 miles from the English coast, the enemy formation was spotted by one of the Spitfire squadrons. The bombers were flying at 18,000 feet, the Me 110's about a thousand feet above them in two waves. The Spitfire squadron was about 3,000 feet higher yet, between the enemy and the sun. By now, the Luftwaffe had a healthy respect for the Spitfires. Spitfire pilots would occasionally pick up the voices of German pilots on their headphones nervously warning, "*Achtung, achtung, Schpitfeuer!*" ("Attention, attention, Spitfire!")

If the Spitfires were surprised by the size of the enemy formation, the Germans were no less surprised by the presence of British fighters at all. For the attack from Norway was launched in the mistaken belief that British fighter planes had been withdrawn from the north to aid the hard-pressed fighter groups in the south.

Despite the odds, the Spitfire squadron attacked swiftly, four of them engaging the Me 110's while the rest dove on the bombers from astern. The results were startling. Some of the bombers quickly dropped their bombs into the sea and sought cover in the clouds. The Me 110's, flying without their rear machine-gunners in order to increase their range, were helpless. They flew in defensive circles to protect themselves, leaving the bombers at the mercy of the Spitfires. According to Group Captain Desmond Sheen, who took part in the action, "much slaughter was inflicted on the enemy."

The enemy formation split up, one part heading south, the other north. Both groups ran into heavy fighter opposition and were forced to drop their bomb loads blindly. Most of the bombs fell harmlessly into the sea. The battered raiders then turned back to their bases in Norway. In all, they had lost eight bombers and seven fighters. Fighter Command did not lose a single plane.

While this action was taking place, Luftflotte 5 was attempting another attack about 90 miles to the south. A flight of 50 Junkers 88's, unescorted by fighters, was headed for a Bomber Command airfield at Driffield. The Ju 88 was a very fast, maneuverable bomber, but it was no match for Spitfires and Hurricanes. Despite heavy fighter opposition, about 30 of the Ju 88's got through to Driffield and bombed the airfield heavily, destroying about a dozen bombers and four hangars. In this action, eight Ju 88's were lost. Fighter Command did not lose any planes.

During the rest of the day, the fighting was more even. A formation of nearly 45 dive-bombers escorted by fighters struck the Fighter Command airfield at Martlesham and got away without a loss. It successfully eluded seven British fighter squadrons sent up to intercept it. Another formation of 100 bombers with fighter escort headed toward eastern Kent. While the German fighter escort engaged four British fighter squadrons, most of the bombers flew on unmolested to bomb two aircraft factories at Rochester and an airfield at Eastchurch, inflicting heavy damage. The Germans lost four fighters in this action, while Fighter Command lost nine.

Using another very large force, the Germans then launched an attack on England's south coast. About 80 bombers, some of them Stukas, accompanied by Me 109's and Me 110's, split up and attacked the town of Portland, an airfield at Middle Wallop, and a Navy airport at Worthy Down. Opposed by large formations of fighters from No. 11 and No. 10 Groups, the Luftwaffe lost heavily. Eight bombers, four dive-bombers, and 13 Me 110's were destroyed. Fighter Command lost 16 planes.

In the final action of the day, between 60 and 70 German planes seriously damaged two aircraft factories and an airfield at Croydon, and another airfield at West Malling. About 80 people were killed or seriously injured in the aircraft factories. In these last attacks, the Luftwaffe lost seven planes, while Fighter Command lost five.

The day's fighting had stretched both sides to the limit, but it was, by every yardstick, a major British victory. Goering had thrown almost everything he had into this battle in an attempt to destroy Fighter Command in the air and its facilities on the ground. He had failed on both counts. The amount of damage inflicted on R.A.F. airfields was, all things considered, relatively small. The Luftwaffe had paid heavily for its few successes, losing 76 planes. Fighter Command lost 34. The attacks from Norway and Denmark by Luftflotte 5 were almost a complete fiasco.

The day's fighting had three major results. Luftflotte 5 was virtually withdrawn from any further daylight fighting. Too late, the Germans had learned that bombers, without an escort of Me 109's, were "sitting ducks" for British fighter planes. And Me 109's did not have enough range to fly from bases in Norway. From this point on, the fighting would be concentrated over southeast England, where Me 109's based near the Channel coast could fly escort. Lastly, it became clear that the Stuka dive-bomber and the Me 110 were badly outmatched against British fighters. A few days later, the Stukas were virtually taken out of the action. The Me 110's would themselves require fighter escorts.

The Germans, however, were not dismayed by the day's results. As usual, Luftwaffe pilots exaggerated British losses wildly. By this time, the Luftwaffe was convinced that Fighter Command had no more than 300 planes left. In reality, it had about 600, although in this period Fighter Command's losses were beginning to exceed replacements. The reserves of fighter planes were thinning and, even more serious, the shortage of pilots was becoming acute. Between August 8 and August 18, Fighter Command had lost 154 pilots killed, missing, and seriously wounded. In the same period, the training schools turned out only 63 new pilots. Some replacements were obtained by recruiting volunteers from among bomber squadrons, the Royal Navy, and other air services. In addition, four new half-squadrons of Polish and Czech airmen were formed. But still these did not nearly meet the overall requirement.

Somehow, despite their heavy losses, the morale of Britain's fighter pilots remained high. They were sure they would not be bested by the Luftwaffe. Many years later, Max Aitken, an ace fighter pilot, told Drew Middleton, author of *The Sky Suspended*:

"I don't think any of us thought we could lose. . . . It just never entered our heads."

Group Captain Norman Ryder recently recalled a typical day of a British fighter pilot:

"Looking back to the Battle of Britain, the most lasting memory is the fantastic unreality of it all. It was a glorious summer, yet the better the weather the greater the tempo of the air battle. Small wonder the Squadron introduced a new cult, 'The Most Dishonorable Order of Fog Worshippers.'

"One day began much like any other. After a night interrupted by the thudding of a battery of antiaircraft guns a few yards away, the lights go on and you struggle out of bed. Downstairs to the anteroom for a cup of tea and a quick telephone call to the Squadron dispersal to find out the number of Spits on the line. Back to the anteroom and there's Ben, fast asleep in an armchair, his head almost resting on his shoulder blade. He hadn't been to bed and was still waiting for his long distance telephone call to his wife to let her know all was well. He didn't know the telephone lines were down. He is still alive and in good health, minus one eye which he lost in the fight a few days later.

"The boys come down one by one. It's barely light as 12 of us clamber into the lorry [truck] outside the Mess, bound for our aircraft. The lorry serves a dual purpose — it also collects the dustbins [garbage cans]. This surely is the

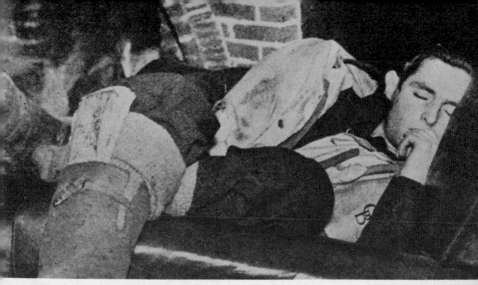

An exhausted British fighter pilot naps in a chair.

lowest ebb of the day. Into flying boots, sweaters, and Mae Wests [inflatable life preserver jackets]. Out to check our aircraft, which look like stranded whales in the half light, and feel like them — cold and dripping wet from the night dew. Back to the crew room and the long tense wait begins. We are 'at readiness.'

"Some play cards, others read, another is trying to teach a dog to stand on one foot, another attacks an ancient set of jazz drums and gets thrown out of the window for his trouble. The burly Flight Sergeant forces his way into the room from time to time and reports the latest state of his aircraft to each pilot. There is still some feeling of security, for we all know it is unlikely we shall be sent into the air before the sun is up. We appreciate the enemy's habits.

"Then we hear it over the loudspeaker: '41 Squadron, SCRAMBLE! Angels 30 — Ashford.' ['Angels 30 — Ashford' meant German planes at 30,000 feet over Ashford — ed.] The room erupts, the dispersal area erupts, the air fills with more and more noise as engine after engine crackles into life. Taxiing out of the dispersal area, a quick check to

77

see if the rest of the Squadron has started up successfully. Yes, 11 Spitfires are moving out behind me, jockeying for their correct take-off positions. . . . A minute later we are airborne from Hornchurch, a fighter airfield some 20 miles east of London. It is a lovely morning, as usual, heralding a cruel day.

"At 20,000 feet I turn into an easterly heading to take full advantage of the sun. I hear the voice of the 'ops' controller in my headphone: 'Firefly Leader, Bandits [Germans] approaching the Dover area, 20 plus, with many more behind.' In the tense silence that follows, everyone strains for that first and vital sighting. . . . 'Eight aircraft coming straight toward us, followed by another eight, and more behind.' We all recognize the voice of 'Hawkeye' Wells, who so consistently lived up to his nickname.

"The enemy does not see our approach and within seconds an orderly scene explodes into a series of unrelated individual actions as each of us selects and attacks an enemy fighter. Suddenly the sky is full of aircraft, and just as suddenly you are on your own. You hunt on your own, or team up with another Spitfire, possibly from another airfield. . . . Out of the corner of your eye you see a 109 burst into flames, then a Spitfire . . . that must be Johnny. So the crazy circus goes on until you are out of ammunition.

"At the airfield, all is ready for a quick refuel and rearm. Aircraft return in dribs and drabs. Some don't return. Claims are made, and so the profit and loss account is totted up.

"Four sorties later, we are released for the day. Just time to get to the pub for a drink with the locals. 'Three pints, please.' Nobody mentions Johnny. 'Cheers!' "

Fighter pilots pass the time waiting for "scramble."

CHAPTER VII
THE LUFTWAFFE
ALMOST WINS
(AUGUST 24–SEPTEMBER 6, 1940)

While the great air battles of August 15 were taking place over Britain, Reichsmarshal Hermann Goering was playing host to his three top Luftwaffe commanders at his country estate in Prussia. Goering was not very happy about the way the overall battle was going, and he proceeded to give his commanders some new directives.

Goering felt that they had been attacking many unessential targets, including factories, thereby diluting their strength. He reminded them that their object was to destroy the Royal Air Force. From now on, he said, they must concentrate on that goal exclusively. Enemy shipping might be attacked under favorable circumstances, but that was the only exception to the rule.

Basically, this was sound advice. But in almost the next breath, Goering made one of his worst blunders. He had never had much respect for Britain's radar stations, considering them to be no more important than weather information stations. He told his commanders that "it is doubtful whether there is any point in continuing the attacks on radar sites, in view of the fact that not one of those attacked so far has been put out of operation." (At that very moment, British technicians were working feverishly to repair the radar station that had been knocked out of action on the Isle of Wight on August 12.) By underestimating the importance of radar stations and thereby limiting further at-

Air Vice-Marshal Keith Park, commander of No. 11 Group.

Goering and Hitler in high spirits after fall of France.

tacks on them, Goering saved Britain's first line of defense against the Luftwaffe. He could not have given the R.A.F. a better present.

Four days later, on August 19, Goering reviewed the situation again with his commanders. This time, he gave them more specific instructions. "We have reached the decisive phase in the air war against England," he said. "Our first aim is the destruction of the enemy's fighters. If they no longer take the air, we shall attack them on the ground or force them into battle by directing bomber attacks against targets within the range of our fighters. . . . Surprise attacks on the enemy aircraft industry must be made by day and by night. Once the enemy air force has been eliminated, our attacks will be directed against other vital targets."

The Luftwaffe soon made plans to carry out the destruction of Fighter Command. It was obvious that the Luftwaffe had not seriously crippled Britain's fighter defenses by attacking the R.A.F.'s forward, or coastal, airfields. Now the Luftwaffe decided to strike at Fighter Command's inland airfields, especially those of No. 11 Group, which guarded London and southeast England. This area, which was closest to the Continent, was within range of the Me 109's. It was also the most likely area to be invaded, in the event "Sea Lion" was carried out. The Luftwaffe's main targets would be Fighter Command's sector stations. The sector stations, equipped with "ops" rooms that guided fighter squadrons once they were airborne, were the nerve centers of Fighter Command. There were seven of them in No. 11 Group. If these could be destroyed, Fighter Command could no longer operate in southeast England. The whole area would then be at the mercy of German bombers and, possibly, invaders.

The Luftwaffe had chosen its targets well this time. It had also worked out more effective tactics, designed to cut down bomber losses. Bombers would no longer fly unescorted by fighters. The ratio of bombers to escort fighters would be much smaller. The bombers would, in a sense, serve as decoys, luring British fighters into combat against the Me 109's. The Me 109's were ordered to give the bomber formations much closer escort than in the past. Originally, they had flown much higher than the bombers. The British had often taken advantage of this by ordering Hurricanes to attack the bomber formations while the faster Spitfires took on the fighter escort. Now the Me 109's were to stay close to the bombers. Me 109 pilots, used to playing an aggressive role, later protested that this strategy limited their mobility in combat. Nevertheless, these new tactics proved effective. British fighters would find it much harder to get through to the bombers in the future.

While the Luftwaffe was devising these new tactics, Keith Park, the commander of No. 11 Group, was also giving some thought to future tactics. Although he was actually unaware of what the Luftwaffe was planning, Park seems to have had a sixth sense about it. Park had two goals: He wanted to engage incoming bombers before they reached their targets and, at the same time, keep his fighter losses to a minimum. He therefore ordered his fighters to concentrate their attacks on the bombers and avoid prolonged combat with enemy fighters. He did not want to "trade off" his fighters against those of the enemy, who had the advantage of numbers. So Park had already decided not to be drawn into any unprofitable combat with enemy fighters. Above all, Park wanted to protect his sector stations from destruction. Large formations of fighters were to maintain constant air patrols whenever the sector stations were in serious danger. If necessary, he would call on fighters from No. 12 Group to guard his sector stations north of the Thames when his own fighters were engaged elsewhere. These were wise precautions, and Park would need every one of them.

From August 19 to August 23, cloudy weather kept the Luftwaffe from mounting heavy attacks. But on the 24th, the weather cleared, and the Luftwaffe struck hard. From that day through September 6, the Luftwaffe relentlessly attacked No. 11 Group's inner airfields and sector stations. Luftwaffe bombers, now carefully guarded by escort fighters, were able to inflict heavy damage on them.

From September 1-6 especially, the situation was grim for

Fighter Command. While its airfields were being battered, pilots and planes were being destroyed much faster than they could be replaced. From August 24 to September 6, 295 fighter planes were totally destroyed and 171 badly damaged. Only 269 new and repaired fighters were sent in as replacements. In the same period, 103 Fighter Command pilots were killed or missing, and 128 were wounded. The training schools could not nearly keep pace with the need. Fresh squadrons, moved in to replace exhausted ones, often suffered heavier losses than those they had replaced. One new squadron went into action on August 28. By September 6, it had lost 16 planes and 12 pilots. British replacement pilots were often easy prey for the more experienced Luftwaffe pilots. As for the experienced Fighter Command pilots, the strain of flying seven or eight sorties a day was producing a terrible weariness in them. It was also rough on their nerves and digestion. Some men became sick to their stomachs almost every time they heard the loudspeaker call "Scramble!" The bright young faces of June, 1940, were now lined and tired. Fighter Command was slowly but surely being bled to death. Only a miracle could save it from destruction.

On August 31, Fighter Command suffered its heaviest losses in planes — 39. The Luftwaffe lost 41 planes, indicating that the score was evening up. Early that morning, waves of German planes flew over southeast England, attacking a number of inner airfields. The one at Debden was hit hardest. A formation of Dornier 17's unloaded about 100 high explosive and incendiary bombs on it, scoring direct hits on barracks, the field hospital, and other buildings. The "ops" room, fortunately, was able to continue functioning. Later, more than 100 German planes bombed the airfield at Eastchurch, damaging buildings and cratering runways.

The most serious attack of the day came soon after noon.

Two views of R.A.F. airfields under attack. *Above:* A Hurricane survives bomb blasts. *Right:* A direct hit.

About 100 German planes crossed the English coast and then split up. One section attacked the airfield at Croydon, destroying a hangar and damaging other buildings. Then it headed for the airfield at Biggin Hill, which had already suffered heavy damage the day before. On that day, August 30, workshops, barracks, offices, W.A.A.F. quarters, a hangar, and other buildings were wrecked. Casualties had been heavy — 39 men and women killed and 26 injured. On the 31st, further damage was done to hangars and buildings, and a direct hit was scored on the "ops" room, setting fires, filling the room with smoke and dust, and knocking out power cables and telephone lines. For a time, Biggin Hill was cut off from all communication with the outside. Because of the extensive damage to the airfield, two of the three fighter squadrons there had to be moved to other fields.

Meanwhile the other Luftwaffe section attacked the airfield at Hornchurch just as a British fighter squadron was taking off. Three of the fighters were struck by bomb blasts and wrecked, yet their pilots miraculously escaped with only superficial injuries. One of them was Flight Lieutenant Alan Deere (who told in Chapter V of the first plane he shot down). In all, about 100 bombs hit the field, cratering it badly.

The last attacks of the day were carried out by Ju 88 bombers and Me 110's carrying bombs. Again the airfield at Hornchurch was hit and two Spitfires were destroyed on the ground.

The loss of Fighter Command pilots during this period was severe, but it would have been worse if some had not been able to bail out of their planes or successfully crash-land them. Many pilots were able to get back into action again, some of them quite quickly. Group Captain Petrus

"Dutch" Hugo survived a crash landing, took a bride.

Hendrik "Dutch" Hugo recently recalled crash-landing his Hurricane:

"About half-past 12," Hugo said, "we were scrambled and . . . ordered to climb to 25,000 feet on a northerly course to intercept enemy fighters. We saw nothing until we were nearly at 25,000 feet when vapor trails appeared high to starboard. . . . I realized that with the sun behind us and enemy fighters above we were sitting targets. Suddenly, almost magically, an Me 109 appeared behind Sgt. Wally, flying No. 2 in Green Section on the extreme starboard. I yelled a warning over the R/T [radio-telephone] and turned sharply to starboard to engage the enemy

89

fighter, but it was already too late. Sgt. Wally's plane burst into flames and before I had more than started to turn all hell broke loose. There was a blinding flash and a deafening explosion in the left side of the cockpit somewhere behind the instrument panel. My left leg received a numbing, sickening blow and a sheet of high octane petrol [gasoline] shot back into the cockpit from the main tank. My stricken Hurricane flicked over into a spin and must have been hit half a dozen times while doing so. . . . The sledge-hammer cracks of cannon and machine gun strikes went on for what seemed ages.

"Without any conscious effort, I had turned off the fuel . . . to decrease the risk of fire — the dreadful bogey of all pilots. Petrol kept gushing into the cockpit and I was soaked through to the skin, but I dared not open the cockpit hood to bail out as the flaming exhaust stubs were glowing right in front of the cockpit and one spark would have turned everything into a blazing inferno. Finally the engine coughed, sputtered, and ceased firing. I put the airscrew [propeller] into coarse pitch and switched off the ignition. The airscrew slowed down until it was just flicking over lazily . . . and I knew the immediate danger of fire was over.

"A sigh of relief and a prayer of thankfulness seemed to be in order as I slowly pulled out of the spin, but both were rather premature. No sooner had the sky and earth returned to their proper places than there was the most colossal bang behind me and the now familiar sound of cannon strikes. I must have got the biggest fright of my life . . . as a particularly vicious-looking Me 109 with a yellow nose snarled about 20 feet past my starboard, the venomous crackle of his Daimler-Benz engine clearly audible. Round he came for another attack and, although I did everything I could think of, gliding without power has its limitations. The next moment earth and sky seemed to explode into crimson flame as I received the most almighty blow on the side of the head.

"I came to, feeling sick and shaken, to find the aircraft spinning comfortably. Through a red haze, I could see that I was still some 10,000 feet up, so I took stock of the situation. My head was aching savagely and the right side of my face felt numb. . . . The cockpit appeared to have lots more ventillation in it than normally and was filled with a fine red spray. It took me some time to realize that blood was pouring over my chest and was being whipped by the wind into a fine spray. The cockpit hood was getting covered inside with a mixture of petrol and blood and was difficult to see through, so I slid it back and gulped in huge lungfuls of clean air. . . ."

Hugo corrected the plane's spin and, because he was running out of altitude, began looking for a field to crash-land in. He found a suitable field, but his landing speed was much too fast and his plane came to a halt violently.

"The nose of the plane dug in and the tail reared up, my chest was smashed against the curving edge of the windscreen and the partnership of pilot and Hurricane finished up in an untidy heap, with me thrown half out of the cockpit. . . . Next moment I was in the clutches of half a dozen cheerful and eager ambulance men who had me wrapped up in bandages till I could hardly breathe, dumped me on a stretcher and trotted off to where their ambulance was parked in the wood a few hundred yards away. Soon afterward, I was on the operating table of the War Emergency Hospital, Orpington, where the gashes on my face were sewn up and a machine-gun bullet removed from my left leg. . . ."

CHAPTER VIII
THE BATTLE
REACHES A CLIMAX
(SEPTEMBER 7–SEPTEMBER 30, 1940)

On September 6, 1940, the Luftwaffe had never stood so close to victory. Fighter Command's losses were becoming disastrous. Slowly but surely, No. 11 Group's sector stations and other airfields were being wrecked. Had the Luftwaffe kept up its attacks on these fields for another week or so, No. 11 Group, the heart of Fighter Command, might well have been finished. That, at least, was the view expressed by Keith Park on the 25th anniversary of the Battle of Britain in 1965. Park said, "Had my fighter airfields been put out of action, the German Air Force would have won the battle by the 15th September."

Dowding and Park needed a miracle at this point if Fighter Command was to survive. They got their miracle. It was presented to them by the Supreme Commander of Germany's armed forces, Adolf Hitler. How it came about is one of those great accidents of fate. To see how it happened we must go back a bit.

Throughout July and most of August, the Luftwaffe had carried out a number of light, scattered night raids over large areas of Britain. These raids had little military value and were designed primarily to harass the British people and undermine their spirits. On August 24, the Germans began their attacks on No. 11 Group's sector stations by day. That night, the Luftwaffe also began a series of much heavier night raids, in which Liverpool became the chief target. (Young readers may be interested in knowing that two fa-

A Heinkel 111 flies over the Thames, London, in 1940.

mous Englishmen — Ringo Starr and John Lennon of the Beatles — were born during the raids on Liverpool, Ringo on July 7, John on October 9.)

On the night of August 24 itself, a number of Luftwaffe bombers, aiming at targets on the outskirts of London, hit the center of the city instead. This was probably the result of a navigational error, which in turn might have been caused by the "jamming" of the planes' Knickebein radio beams.

Hitler had forbidden the Luftwaffe to bomb London at this time. His order was not based on any feelings of humanity. He simply felt that the bombing of London was his trump card, which he would play when the right time came. A German High Command directive of August 16 indicated that the bombing of London would take place immediately before the planned invasion. Its purpose would be "to cause the population to flee from the city and block the roads."

Winston Churchill did not know that the bombing of London on the night of August 24 was accidental. He thought it was deliberate and promptly ordered Bomber Command to strike back at Berlin the next night, August 25. That night, 81 R.A.F. bombers carried out a raid on the German capital. Further raids were carried out on Berlin for several nights afterward.

Though they caused little damage, these raids infuriated Hitler. Goering had publicly stated, and Hitler had often implied, that Berlin would never be bombed. On September 4, Hitler made a speech in which he promised that reprisal raids would be made on London. While his audience cheered, Hitler stormed:

"If they attack our cities, we will rub out their cities from the map. The hour will come when one of us two will break and it will not be Nazi Germany!"

Then Hitler warned Britain that an invasion was indeed coming. This is what he said:

"When people are very curious in Great Britain and ask, 'Yes, but why doesn't he come?' we reply: 'Calm yourselves! Calm yourselves! He is coming! He is coming!' "

Hitler's decision to bomb London was formed in anger and was not based on any military considerations. Yet it was supported by some of his top Luftwaffe commanders who thought it was a good idea in terms of strategy. On September 3, Hermann Goering met with Field Marshals Sperrle and Kesselring to discuss the Fuehrer's new plan. Sperrle argued against it. He believed that Fighter Command was still very strong — in fact, he very much exaggerated its strength — and urged a continuation of the attacks on the sector stations. Kesselring, however, believed that Fighter Command had "next to nothing left" and in this he was supported by the top Luftwaffe intelligence officer, Major Josef Schmid. Kesselring argued that the way to finish off Fighter Command was to draw all its remaining planes into battle over London. Goering was impressed with this reasoning and the decision to bomb London was confirmed. The date was set: the attack would begin on September 7.

For Dowding and Park, the decision could not have been a better one. It meant that their sector stations and airfields, which were being battered to bits, would be saved from destruction. While the Luftwaffe switched its attack to London, there would be time to patch up the airfields, operations rooms, and telephone lines. Fighter Command would be able to continue the battle — and win.

For London, of course, Hitler's decision would mean the beginning of a terrible ordeal in which almost 20,000 people would be killed. But London showed that it could "take it," despite its dreadful losses, and in the end Hitler's decision would prove to be his undoing.

September 7 was another fine, sunny, summer day, and, as it was a Saturday, Londoners were taking advantage of the good weather. They had no idea that the Luftwaffe that day was gathering more than 370 bombers and about 640 fighters for an attack on their city. At about 5 o'clock in the afternoon, Hermann Goering and Albert Kesselring stood on the Channel coast and, peering through binoculars, watched their formations fly towards the great city. Fighter Command was caught off balance by the attack. It had fully expected a continuation of the raids on its sector stations, and had planned its defenses accordingly. As a result, the first German formations were able to reach their targets before British fighter planes could intercept.

The first wave of German planes came in from the east and blasted an arsenal and two factories. This was at 5:15. Minutes later, this force was met by seven British fighter squadrons and suffered heavy losses. But while this action was taking place, other German formations were bombing the docks and oil installations along the Thames River almost without interference. Meanwhile, more and more Luftwaffe formations kept coming in from the east. British fighters engaged them in running battles, but generally the German fighter escorts were able to beat them off and allow the bombers to reach their targets. Over three hundred tons of high explosive bombs, and thousands of incendiaries, rained down on the East End docks and on the flimsy, old, two-story slum dwellings that faced them. By 6:30, when the attack halted, most of these slum dwellings were nothing more than dust and rubble, as were the "pubs" and shops among them.

The Luftwaffe had lost 40 planes in the attack, while Fighter Command had lost 28, but the Germans had done extensive damage to London, especially to its East End.

A street goes up in flames during night raid on London.

Even worse, huge fires had been started there. When the sun set, the blaze was visible for miles.

That evening, while firemen were desperately battling the flames, the Germans returned. This time, they had an easy time of it. Guided by the huge fires, they were able to bomb the city almost at will for nearly seven hours. For at night London was virtually without defenses. The British had only two experimental planes equipped with radar for night fighting, and these were much too primitive to be of any real value. They did not engage the attackers at all. Three Blenheim fighter-bombers, without radar, also patrolled the air, but their crews were simply unable to see the enemy in the dark. As for the Spitfires and Hurricanes, they were practically useless at night and did not even attempt opposition.

That left the defense of London chiefly to the antiaircraft guns. There weren't nearly enough of these, and guided only by sound locators that were almost totally ineffective,

97

These London row houses were reduced to rubble by a German raid.

all they could do was fire blindly into the sky. That night, the Germans dropped an even heavier load of bombs than they had during the day, and almost every part of London was hit. More than 250 Luftwaffe bombers took part in the action, but not one was brought down. By the end of that day and night, about 1,000 Londoners had been killed.

While the bombers were cruising over the helpless city, enormous fires were burning out of control. A member of the Women's Voluntary Service, Mrs. Nancy Spender, was sent into the burning East End dock area with an ambulance. This is how she described the fire there in Constantine Fitz Gibbon's book, *The Winter of the Bombs*:

"As far as we could see, everything was on fire. Great red flames were going up and down the brick walls, piles of houses all collapsed or on fire, warehouses like blazing cathedrals standing up and falling down, bricks going up, bombs coming down. There was a most terrific muddle of

Despite such damage, Londoners kept going.

fire, everything reflected in the water. . . . Well, by now
we were in a complete jam — there was nothing but fire-
fighting apparatus, ambulances, hosepipes, the whole thing
a complete and utter traffic jam. . . . We edged along. On
every side roofs fell in with the most terrific explosions, gas
mains blew up, there were constant bangings of bombs and
antiaircraft guns, but it was quite impossible to feel
frightened because it was all on such an enormous scale.
Every few minutes one of those blazing piles shot like a
fountain into the sky. . . .

"Then my driver had an inspiration and he left the road
completely and cut across the wharf. Now we were in a
sort of maze of cinder tracks and little truck lines going
here and there and nothing but hosepipes and fire people
fighting the fires. They were awfully good, and they gave
us pushes to get us over the worst debris. Then we came to
a place that seemed to be a sheet of flame, but my driver

said, 'Oh, I think this is nothing much, we'll get through this,' and he put a terrific spurt on and we got through it and that was all right. Well, then we came to a whole group of firemen, all wearing masks, fighting one of the warehouses which was blazing, and I said to one of them, 'Anyone hurt here?' He said, 'No, all dead, go on.'

"So we went on. . . . Then we asked a man, 'Is this right for Oriental Road?' 'Oriental Road,' he said, 'that's absolutely hopeless, it's ablaze from end to end, you'll never get there.' Well, we did, we went on and then we left the worst of the fire behind us, and quite shortly we came to a little sort of deserted village . . . with two-story houses and not a house had a roof, just a little pub without anything on top of it, a lamp-post right across the road, enormous craters, and in each crater there seemed to be a burning jet, gas main or something which had broken. We had an awful job to get by because the craters were so big and the road was so narrow and half the time we had two wheels on the pavement and two wheels over the crater.

"We went on for a bit and then we came to another road and there wasn't a single house standing — there was nothing, nothing at all except holes. Out of several of these holes little people popped their heads. I said, 'Is this Oriental Road?' And they shouted, 'The ambulance?' And I said, 'Yes, anybody hurt?' They said, 'Over in the shelter.' So then we tried to go on and they said, 'Oh, you can't get your ambulance there, there's no possible road.' So we left the ambulance and I got out a stretcher and we went over to the shelter and put our heads in.

"I suppose there were about 40 people there. I said, 'Anybody hurt?' and not a soul answered. . . . So I went up to

Smoke, flames rise at night from bombed London buildings.

one woman and tapped her and said, 'Is there anybody hurt here?' and she said, 'Over there there's a mother and a two-day-old baby, they've both been dug out, and I think further up there's a boy with a very bad knee, he was buried up to his waist, but I don't know about the others.' So I went over to the mother. She didn't speak, and I wrapped her in a blanket and put her on the stretcher, and I said, 'Is there a Warden here?' and somebody said, 'No, he was killed half an hour ago.' So I got a couple of men anyway to help me and we took her back on the stretcher and put her in the ambulance. Then I came back again and collected the boy, with some help, and after that I just filled the ambulance with as many people as I could cram in, about 15 or 16. Still nobody spoke, it was all the most deathly silence. . . . Anyway we got them all back and we got them to the hospital and we got back to our station I suppose about half past one in the morning."

While such terrible scenes were taking place in London, Hermann Goering was speaking over the German radio, congratulating himself:

"This is the historic hour when for the first time our air force delivered its thrust right into the enemy's heart."

But Goering was wrong. Despite the fires and the serious damage, London had not been dealt a mortal blow, not on that night or on any night to come. London was hurt, but the city was much too large, and its people far too courageous, for the Luftwaffe to be able to deliver a fatal blow. London continued to function and to inspire all of Britain throughout the almost continuous bombing it was to suffer in the next two months.

The night of September 7 was notable for one other event related to the bombing of London. The British Chiefs of Staff believed that the bombing of the capital meant that the Germans were about to launch an invasion of England at any moment. After a meeting with Prime Minister Winston Churchill, it was decided to put all the armed forces in a state of instant readiness. Therefore, at eight o'clock that evening, the code word "Cromwell" was sent out, signifying that an invasion was imminent. Unfortunately, many officers did not know what "Cromwell" meant. They thought it meant that an invasion was actually taking place, and all over England that night there was a great deal of confusion. Church bells were rung by the Home Guard, signaling an invasion, road blocks were closed, some cars were shot at, bridges were blown up, and soldiers and sailors stood at their guns. The next morning, the whole country was buzzing with rumors that an invasion attempt had actually been made, but that it had been hurled back by the Navy and the R.A.F.

The "invasion" was, of course, purely imaginary. Yet there were many reasons, besides "Cromwell," why the British might have thought it was real. After his discussions with Admiral Raeder on July 31, Hitler had set September 15 as the tentative date for launching "Sea Lion" — the invasion of England. Everything hinged on the ability of the Luftwaffe to knock out the R.A.F. by that time. In the meanwhile, the German Navy was given the job of rounding up an invasion fleet. The German Navy did its job well. During the first week of September, British reconnaissance planes spotted large numbers of barges, tugs, and troop transports gathering in the Channel ports of Holland, Belgium, and northern France. On September 5, British bombers began to concentrate their attacks on these ports, and inflicted a good deal of damage on the invasion fleet. On clear nights, some of the fires they set could be seen along the south coast of England. So the English people knew something was up.

These attacks by Bomber Command may have given

Hitler some pause for thought. Obviously, the R.A.F. had *not* been knocked out of action. Not yet, anyway. By this time, at the request of the German Navy, the invasion date had been set back until September 21. Because the Navy required 10 days to make its preparations, Hitler had to confirm the invasion date on September 11. On that day, the Fuehrer announced that he wanted three more days to think it over. On September 13, Admiral Raeder told Hitler that Goering had failed to "provide conditions for carrying out the operation." On the 14th, Hitler put off his decision again until the 17th. (That meant that the invasion could not take place earlier than September 27.) Because of the uncertain situation in the air, Hitler said, the moment to launch "Sea Lion" had not yet come. So everything still depended on knocking out the R.A.F. and especially Fighter Command. Hitler had one other hope — that the bombing of London might even make "Sea Lion" unnecessary. Hitler expressed his opinion that week that "the English may yet be seized with mass hysteria" and give in. Again he sadly underestimated the British people.

Despite his hesitation, Hitler was still quite optimistic at this point. Both he and the German High Command believed that Fighter Command was at the end of its rope and that air supremacy might be won at any moment. There was a widespread belief, nourished by exaggerated Luftwaffe claims, that Fighter Command had no more than 100 planes left. (Actually, thanks to increased production, the figure was closer to 600.) "Four or five more days of good weather and a decisive result will be achieved," Hitler said on the 14th. All that was needed was one more big effort. The Luftwaffe decided to make it on September 15.

September 15 is now celebrated every year in Great Britain as "Battle of Britain Day." On that day in 1940, Fighter Command won its most decisive victory in the entire battle. August 15 had shown the German High Command that air supremacy could not be won in a few days. September 15 persuaded it that air supremacy probably would not be won at all. It was the climax of the Battle of Britain and the first turning point in the war against Germany.

The Luftwaffe began massing its formations over the coast of France at about 11 o'clock on the morning of September 15. The bombers — Heinkel 111's, Dornier 17's, and Junkers 88's — picked up their fighter escorts, the Me 109's and Me 110's, as they gained altitude. Once more, the Luftwaffe's planning went awry. Too much time was spent assembling the formations, thereby giving British radar stations ample warning that something very big was going on. Furthermore, the Germans did not make their usual feints to draw off part of Fighter Command's forces. As a result, Fighter Command was able to get a large number of fighter squadrons into the air in time to meet the threat.

By the time the German formations crossed the southeast coast of England, Fighter Command had 17 squadrons in the air ready to intercept. There were 11 squadrons from No. 11 Group, five from No. 12 Group, and one from No. 10 Group. The five squadrons from No. 12 Group flew in one big "wing," a favorite strategy of the group's commander, Air Vice-Marshal Leigh-Mallory. They were led by the intrepid fighter ace, Douglas "Tin Legs" Bader. The squadrons from No. 11 Group flew in pairs, a favorite strategy of that group's commander, Air Vice-Marshal Keith Park.

These squadrons gave the German formations a warm reception. Two Spitfire squadrons pounced on the first German formations of 60-70 planes each over Canterbury and were soon joined by three more. While they were engaging the enemy, Park decided to send six more squadrons into action, squadrons that he had been holding in reserve.

All over southeast England, crowds on the ground were watching the air battles as they developed, and for once the R.A.F. did not seem to be very badly outnumbered. Though beset by fighter squadrons almost all the way, the German formations flew steadily on toward London, closing ranks when one of their bombers was shot down. Over London, they were attacked by the five squadrons of No. 12 Group led by Douglas Bader.

Bader's memories of this day, and similar ones, are, he says, "kaleidoscopic." As he recalls them:

"Two Hurricanes converging on the same Junkers 88. You cannot shout a warning because you are not carrying their radio frequency. The Hurricanes touch, a wing breaks off, and falls away like a falling leaf. One pilot bails out and lands safely to live to continue the fight another day. You are closing in on a Dornier 17 when some sixth sense makes you look up to see a Spitfire diving vertically from above. As you sheer away the Spitfire hits the Dornier squarely in the middle. It wraps itself around the fighter and they both go down on fire and seemingly quite slowly, like a ball of paper that has been set alight and thrown into the air. It was not an intentional ram. The Spitfire pilot had been firing at another enemy and had not seen the Dornier below him. A stream of bullets crashes into the dashboard of your aircraft and you nearly die of fright as you wrench it around. You see the Messerschmitt that nearly got you go past in an ever-steepening dive with the Hurricane that has killed it on its tail. As you watch, the Messerschmitt disappears into the pall of smoke from the burning oil tanks at Shell Haven on the north bank of the Thames estuary. . . ."

Winston Churchill boards boat to inspect London dock area.

The five squadrons of No. 12 Group and other squadrons did their job so well that the Germans were forced to drop their bombs helter-skelter. As a result, the damage they did was not very serious. One bomb did fall on the grounds of Buckingham Palace, but it failed to explode. Their ranks heavily riddled, the German formations finally returned to their bases, but not before being mauled by four more British fighter squadrons on the way back.

Two hours later, there was a second and heavier attack on London. Fighter Command benefited by the interval, being able to refuel and rearm its squadrons in time to meet the second wave of attackers. This time there was not quite as much warning as in the morning, but still No. 11 Group was able to get six pairs of squadrons into the air while the Germans were still over the Channel. Soon after, No. 11 Group put up another seven and a half squadrons while No. 12 Group again sent five squadrons into action in a single "wing." No. 10 Group again sent up one squadron. In all, twenty-five and a half squadrons went up to meet the enemy, an even greater force than in the morning.

The attackers flew toward London in three formations. One was intercepted near Canterbury by two Spitfire squadrons that were later joined by Hurricanes. Further west, another German formation ran into two Hurricane squadrons. The Hurricanes swarmed all over the formation, forcing part of it to dump its bombs and turn back to its bases. Most of the action took place over London, where five pairs of squadrons from No. 11 Group and the wing from No. 12 Group took on the third German formation and survivors of the first two. The enemy dropped a big

Hurricane fighters on the lookout for German planes.

bomb load on the city and scored several lucky hits on railroads and public utilities. But the damage that day was not nearly as severe as that inflicted on September 7.

At the height of the battle on the 15th, Keith Park had an important visitor at his Group Headquarters. The visitor was none other than Winston Churchill, who made a habit of visiting his Group commanders often. Churchill recorded his visit to Park's headquarters on this day in his book, *Their Finest Hour*. At one point Churchill noted that, despite Park's outward calm, all his fighter squadrons were in the air and not a single one was left in reserve. Park then called Dowding at Fighter Command Headquarters and requested three more squadrons from No. 12 Group to be put at his disposal to meet any new attack while his squadrons were refueling and rearming. This was done. Nevertheless, Churchill noticed that Park still looked worried. This is how Churchill described the scene:

"I became conscious of the anxiety of the Commander, who now stood still behind his subordinate's chair. Hitherto I had watched in silence. I now asked, 'What other reserves have we?' 'There are none,' said Air Vice-Marshal Park. In an account which he wrote about it afterward, he said that at this I 'looked grave.' Well I might. What losses should we not suffer if our refuelling planes were caught on the ground by further raids of '40 plus' or '50 plus'! The odds were great; our margins small; the stakes infinite."

Despite the odds and the small margins the British won the day. By the end of it, after two other diversion raids by the Luftwaffe, Fighter Command had lost 26 planes. The Luftwaffe had lost 60. The loss of 60 planes, added to about 140 others the Luftwaffe had lost since September 7, was a stunning blow to the Germans. Even the Luftwaffe could not afford to lose planes at such a rate. Furthermore, Fighter Command had shown conclusively that it was *not* about to be driven from the air. The Luftwaffe commanders, once supremely confident, were now shaken. The German Navy, never keen on invading England, was now even less keen. The Army, confident earlier that it could do its part once the Luftwaffe had won air supremacy, was now having doubts of its own.

Hitler had told the German High Command that he would make his decision on an invasion of Britain on September 17. He did. His decision was recorded in the war diary of the German Navy:

"The enemy air force is still by no means defeated. On the contrary, it shows increasing activity. The weather situation as a whole does not permit us to expect a period of calm [on the English Channel]. . . . *The Fuehrer therefore decides to postpone Sea Lion indefinitely.*"

And so Britain was spared the ordeal of an invasion, although it did not know it at the time. Gradually, the German invasion fleet was withdrawn from the Channel ports and dispersed. On September 18 there were more than 1,000 invasion craft in these ports. By the end of October, there were only 448 left. On October 12, Hitler told his High Command in a secret order that "preparations for Sea Lion shall be continued solely for the purpose of maintaining political and military pressure on England." In short, Sea Lion was now only a bluff. Although Hitler said the invasion might be reconsidered "in the spring or early summer" of 1941, he was never again able to menace Britain with an invasion. He had had his chance and lost.

Britain had been saved chiefly by about 1,000 boys and young men who flew for Fighter Command. In the words of Prime Minister Winston Churchill, spoken on August 20, 1940:

"Never in the field of human conflict was so much owed by so many to so few."

111

CHAPTER IX
LONDON'S ORDEAL: "THE BLITZ"
(SEPTEMBER 7–NOVEMBER 13, 1940)

Hitler had called off "Sea Lion," but that did not mean that he had abandoned hope of defeating Britain by continued air attacks on its cities. Hitler still nurtured the dream that bombing would terrorize the British people and make them sue for peace. Therefore the air attacks were kept up, by day and by night. Gradually, however, there was a change in the Luftwaffe's tactics. Because of the great losses it had suffered in large daylight raids, it began to concentrate on bombing at night, when the British defenses were still extremely weak. (Radar-equipped and guided night-fighter planes and antiaircraft guns did not become effective forces until the following year.) Daylight raids were still made, but more and more they were executed by small formations of fast fighter planes carrying relatively light bomb loads. By October 1, regular bombers were assigned almost entirely to night raids. Most of the night raids were made on London, but other cities were also bombed occasionally after dark.

The British call this period, when the Luftwaffe concentrated on bombing London by night, "the Blitz." They tend to separate it from "the Battle of Britain," which they see as the great air war that took place by day until, approximately, the 18th of September, when the last big daylight raid on London was made. Yet "the Blitz" was very much a part of the overall battle, and the courage of Londoners throughout their long ordeal shattered Hitler's

London buildings, damaged by bombs, are dynamited.

hopes that Britain might surrender without an invasion.

It *was* a long ordeal. From September 7 until November 13, London was attacked almost every night by an average of 160 German bombers. The heaviest attacks came on bright, moonlit nights, when the Germans could see their target easily. The heaviest raid of all came on the night of October 15, when more than 400 bombers dropped about 540 tons of explosives on the city, killing 400 people and seriously injuring 800 more. More than 900 fires were started, and extensive damage was done to railroads, and to gas and water mains, as well as to homes. Winston Churchill later wrote:

"Our outlook at this time was that London, except for its strong, modern buildings, would be gradually and soon reduced to a rubble heap."

What was life like in London during the Blitz? It was a time of tragedy, and yet it was also a time of remarkably good spirits and fellowship, when people of all classes drew

raid of December 29, 1940. View from roof of St. Paul's.

together to help each other in their common peril. Altogether, nearly 20,000 people were killed and 25,000 seriously injured in London from September, 1940, to May, 1941, when the Blitz finally ended. Such figures, however, cannot convey the calamity that is the loss of even one life for those to whom it was dear. To understand fully the horror of the Blitz, listen to this cleaning woman's story, recounted in Constantine Fitz Gibbon's book, *The Winter of the Bombs*:

"There was Mother, she was an invalid in bed, and Father was an invalid in bed, and we had this time bomb, you see, at the back of the garden, and the wardens came round and said we'd have to evacuate the house and take shelter elsewhere. So they put us underneath the railway arch, and we all slept there, and of course it was rather cold and damp. Then a gentleman came along, after about three nights, and he said, 'There's a billiard hall around the corner,' and the gentleman said, 'if you care to go in there, since

115

there's only a few of you, you can go in the hall.' And naturally we all went and we got quite one really good happy family.

"So we made little beds on the floor for the children, and made them quite comfortable and didn't hear a sound of a night time of anything coming over. Until one night, when there was a great crash, and of course one or two of them got scared. Then a couple of 'em said, 'Well, let's have a little singsong.' So we had a nice little singsong, quieted the children down again, and some of the men played billiards, and then the women said, 'Well, shall we try and get a little nap ourselves?' So we tried to have a little nap ourselves, and then another little kiddie woke up. 'Is there really anything coming, Mummy?' 'Oh no, no, now go to sleep,' she says, 'it's quite all right.' Off to sleep they went again, and of course nothing happened that night, and nothing the next night, and it was quite all right.

"And of course then when the big night came it was really awful, one great crash and a big flash, and there was a stampede of one or two of them trying to get out, and they couldn't get out, and then there was a big fire in the shelter, and then I had the misfortune — I lost my mother in there, and I lost my little girl in there.

"And we had to wait, oh three or four days before we could find either. We went to the hospitals and couldn't find them, no, nothing there. Then I went around to the baths, and they says: 'Well, why don't you go to the mortuary?' Naturally I went round there, and when I got there they just had one there. They asked me to describe my mother, and I did, and it wasn't my mother at all. And then I spoke about my daughter. He says: 'How old is she?' I said: 'She was eight years old.' So he said: 'Well, we have one little girl here,' he says, 'not identified.' And when I looked, I'd never seen such a shock in all my life. All her little hair was burned, and her face where she'd put her fingers right across, all the fire was there, and I thought: 'Oh dear now, can it be true?' Then I thought to myself: 'Well, I suppose the Lord's taken her, you know, to be right out of pain altogether,' and I thought to myself, 'well, I'd sooner her go that way than be maimed for life, you know, a little cripple.'

"And then I thought to myself: 'Well, what about my mother?' And we never did find anything of Mother at all. And I don't think a day goes by without we don't think of my mother and my little daughter. It was the Lord's way to take her, and not be injured, you know, and I still think we've got her with us, you see.' "

This, and thousands of other stories like it, was the tragic side of the Blitz. Yet there *was* another side. The people of London, of all classes, became much friendlier than ever before or, perhaps, ever since. Englishmen, especially those of the middle class, guard their privacy jealously, and tend to be quite reserved. People who live next door to each other for years may never exchange any other words than "Good morning," or "Lovely day, isn't it?"

All that changed during the Blitz. People were thrown together with their neighbors, and even perfect strangers, in numerous situations — in air raid shelters, first-aid stations, fire-fighting groups, and groups to repair each other's homes. And there was so much to talk about. Mainly they talked about the bombs — the ones that didn't go off, the ones that just missed, the ones that kept ticking away, the ones that fell on Buckingham Palace and St. Paul's Cathedral. They praised or damned their air raid wardens, carped about people who violated the blackout regulations, and pitied those who had suffered misfortune. Everyone had a story to tell, and in the "pubs" after a bad raid people took turns to tell theirs. And so the old reserve broke

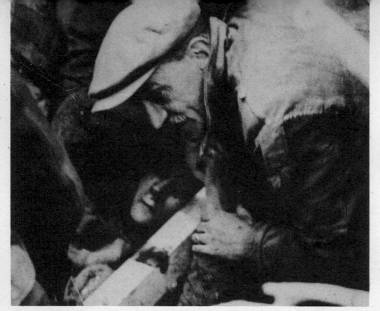

Rescue squad digs out a woman bomb victim in London.

down and perfect strangers not only talked to each other
but shared cabs and bought each other drinks.

People showed their friendship in other ways, too. They
looked after each other's children, shared their stoves
with their less fortunate neighbors, and lent each other all
kinds of necessities. There was kindness, there was sym-
pathy, and there was understanding.

Where did Londoners seek shelter during these nightly
raids? Today we are inclined to think that practically all
of them slept at night on subway station platforms and in
other large, public shelters. The fact is, most Londoners
chose to sleep at home, when they had one. Usually they
put their beds in basements, or under staircases, or in hall-
ways, where they were partially protected against bomb
blasts. Many of these people were motivated by pride. To
spend the night in a shelter, though it might be much safer,
was an admission of fear, and this they would not permit
themselves. "If I'm going to die, I'm going to die in my own

St. Paul's Cathedral suffered a direct hit during Blitz.

house," one upper-class Londoner said. "No shelter for me."

Of those people who did spend the nights in shelters, most preferred their own private shelters, which were built half underground; less than 10 per cent slept in public shelters such as large cellars, brick shelters on streets, and trench shelters in parks; less than five per cent slept on the subway platforms.

Yet it was the subway shelters that got the most attention and the most publicity. At first, the British government opposed the use of subway stations as air raid shelters. It feared that many people in them might panic and refuse to come out at all. Also, since the stations were without sanitary facilities, they might breed epidemics. But it was almost impossible to keep people from using the subway stations at night. They *seemed* so safe. (Only the very deep ones actually were.) Those who did use them were mostly working class people whose homes had been bombed out and who had no other place to go.

Some Londoners slept on subway platforms to escape raids.

In the beginning, these subway shelters were terribly uncomfortable. Thousands of people crammed into them, sleeping on mattresses, blankets, and other makeshift bedding. Each family or group eventually "reserved" its own particular spot on the platform, and soon got to know its neighbors really well. ("Hope them bloomin' Jerries get it tonight, Joe, for all they've done to us.")

By seven in the evening, the younger children were already tucked in while the adults were eating sandwiches, or drinking tea out of thermos bottles. At nine, the adults would begin dozing off, many of them sitting up against the wall.

Besides the overcrowding, the hardness of the stone platforms, and the cold, there were other disagreeable aspects to these shelters — lice and the smell of sweat and human excrement.

Eventually, the government changed its attitude toward these shelters and decided to make them as clean and comfortable as possible. Sanitary facilities were installed, the stations were regularly sprayed with antiseptic, and stoves were put in to provide heat. Soon after, regular bunks were built to make sleeping more comfortable and to eliminate overcrowding. The aged, the sick, and children were sent to hospitals and homes in the country.

After a while, the subway shelters became almost cozy. Some of them acquired pianos and there was singing and dancing. Amateur actors toured the shelters, books and phonographs were provided, lectures given, and movies shown. For some of the slum dwellers, whose homes had often been much worse, the subway shelters were "not so bad, y' know."

The subway shelterers did *not* panic, and in the morning they promptly left the stations to go to work. In fact, instances of panic were very rare in London throughout the entire period of the Blitz. While Hitler hoped for "mass hysteria," and the British government feared it, the people themselves remained remarkably calm and cheerful. During the Blitz, the number of Londoners with mental disorders actually declined. There were also fewer suicides, much less drunkenness, and less disorderly conduct. As Constantine Fitz Gibbon put it, "The Blitz not only did not drive the people mad, but apparently kept quite a few of them sane."

The courage shown by Londoners during the Blitz was emulated by Britons in other cities, many of which came under savage attack by the Luftwaffe around the middle of November. This new phase of the air war was prompted by Goering's and Hitler's disappointment with the results of the night attacks on London. These had failed to break the spirit of the British people and end their will to fight. Perhaps, Goering thought, the answer lay in hammering at other cities, particularly those with important war indus-

German attack on Coventry left center of city in ruins.

tries. London would be included on the list of targets, but it would not be hit as frequently as in the past.

This new — and last — phase of the air war began on the night of November 14 with a devastating attack on the city of Coventry. Guided by new radio target-finding equipment that replaced Knickebein, about 450 bombers dropped some 500 tons of high explosive bombs and nearly 900 incendiaries on the city. In theory, at least, their targets were various factories within Coventry, but houses and shops were hit, too, and these burned swiftly. Within an hour, the center of Coventry was a sea of fire, visible for miles. About 550 people were killed in the attack that night, which left much of the city in ruins.

Thereafter the Luftwaffe shifted its attacks. On some nights, London still got it. On the night of December 29, for example, incendiary bombs started the greatest fire in the history of London since the great fire of 1666. On other nights, Liverpool, Birmingham, Plymouth, Glasgow,

Bristol, Portsmouth, Southampton, and Belfast were on the receiving end. And yet, while the people of these cities suffered terrible hardships, their spirits were never broken and, if anything, they were more determined than ever to fight Hitler. Furthermore, the Luftwaffe had failed to deal a mortal blow to any of these cities or to their industries.

Perhaps Hitler began to perceive all this himself. As early as September 18 — one day after he had called off "Sea Lion" — Hitler indicated that he was already looking for new fields to conquer. On that day, he issued a new War Directive, No. 21, calling for an invasion of Soviet Russia. The directive began:

"The German Armed Forces must be prepared even before the end of the war against England to overthrow Soviet Russia in a rapid campaign. . . ."

More and more, an invasion of Russia, rather than Britain, became Hitler's great ambition. Possibly he believed that a war against Russia's "Slavic hordes" would be easier than an invasion of Britain. In this, he was to be disappointed, too. In any event, in January, 1941, Hitler summoned his commanders and told them that the invasion of Britain was to be abandoned. Their next objective would be Soviet Russia.

Bombing attacks against British cities were continued, however, although they were limited by bad weather in January and February. In the spring, they were stepped up again. But in May and June, two thirds of the Luftwaffe forces confronting Britain were withdrawn in preparation for the attack on Russia, which began on June 22, 1941. The last raid on London took place on the night of May 10. Six nights later, Birmingham was bombed. This was the last major raid on a British city by the Luftwaffe in World War II. Britain's ordeal was over at last. The Battle of Britain had ended.

CHAPTER X
WHY BRITAIN
WON

The Battle of Britain was the decisive turning point in the history of World War II. It was Hitler's first great defeat, and one from which he would never recover. How did the British manage to win the battle in spite of the great odds against them? A number of widely different elements account for it:

1. On the level of technology, the Royal Air Force was far in advance of the Luftwaffe. Its radar chain was invaluable, enabling British fighter pilots to get into the air and intercept enemy formations often before they could reach their targets. The R.A.F.'s radio ground control system also gave it a much greater flexibility in air battles than the Luftwaffe, which generally had to stick with a prearranged plan of attack. The R.A.F.'s fighter planes were also much more maneuverable than the Luftwaffe's and, armed with eight machine guns, were capable of a greater hail of fire.

2. The Luftwaffe was not really created for the kind of air warfare it was called on to fight in the Battle of Britain. Built primarily to support German ground forces, it could not possibly do *all* the things it was asked to do against Britain — knock out the R.A.F., destroy Britain's industries, attack its shipping, level its cities, and so on. A top Luftwaffe Commander, General Werner Kriepe, recently put it this way:

"The German Air Force was technically not constructed to wage war at extreme range and across salt water. . . . Lacking any clear objective laid down by the Supreme

Prime Minister Winston Churchill inspired his people.

Command, the Luftwaffe was almost bled to death, and suffered losses which could never again be made good in the course of the war. . . . It was a battle that should never have been fought at all. The decision to fight it marks a turning point in the history of the Second World War."

3. Winston Churchill gave the British people brilliant leadership. He inspired them to resist the onslaught of the world's most powerful dictatorship, and to prove that a democracy could more than hold its own in such a struggle. Hitler and Goering gave Germany very poor leadership. Goering's decision to discontinue the attacks on the British radar system was a major blunder. And Hitler's decision to bomb London, seconded by Goering, was an even greater mistake, possibly the costliest — to them — of the war.

4. Not enough can be said for "the few" — the pilots of Fighter Command who never considered defeat and who outdid themselves in combat, knowing all along that theirs was a just cause.

Consider this tribute recently paid "the few" by Mrs. Anne Turley George, a member of the W.A.A.F. during the Battle of Britain, and the wife of a former fighter pilot:

"We lay in ditches and watched the dogfights and cheered on our warriors and laughed and danced and sang with them in the evenings, and saw them off the next day with the tight fist of fear knotted deep in our insides — and more and more fell . . . and all of them so young and so well endowed, and such a wicked, wicked waste. I mourned them then, now, and forever. . . . They held our lives, our happiness, and our heritage in their young strong hands and they never flinched. I wish I could write music — I would create one great triumphant shout of a hymn, praising and honoring them and telling of our love and gratitude to them for ever and ever. Amen."

Former Air Chief Marshal Dowding was reunited in 1969 at age 87 with some of his Battle of Britain aces.